A Little Brother to the Bear

"A fierce battle in the tree-tops"

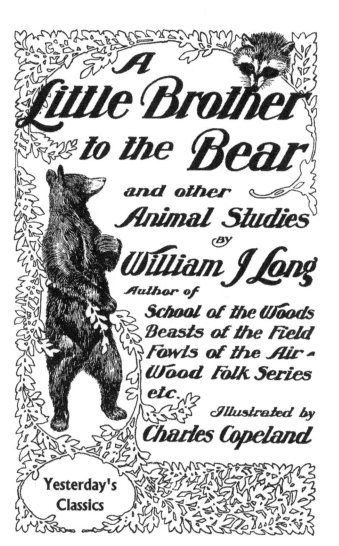

A Little Brother to the Bear

and other Animal Studies

by William J Long

Author of

School of the Woods
Beasts of the Field
Fowls of the Air
Wood Folk Series
etc.

Illustrated by
Charles Copeland

Yesterday's
Classics

This edition, first published in 2006 by
Yesterday's Classics, is an unabridged
republication of the work originally published
by Ginn and Company in 1903. For a complete
listing of books published by Yesterday's
Classics, visit www.yesterdaysclassics.com.
Yesterday's Classics is the publishing arm of the
Baldwin Project which presents the complete
text of dozens of classic books for children at
www.mainlesson.com under the editorship of
Lisa M. Ripperton and T. A. Roth.

ISBN-10: 1-59915-189-8

ISBN-13: 978-1-59915-189-2

Yesterday's Classics
PO Box 3418
Chapel Hill, NC 27515

To Lois, who likes Bears, I dedicate this book of the Bear and his little brother.

Preface

HE object of this little book, so far as it has an object beyond that of sharing a simple pleasure of mine with others, will be found in the first chapter, entitled "The Point of View"; and the title will be explained in the chapter on "A Little Brother to the Bear" that follows.

All the sketches here are reproduced from my own note-books largely, or from my own memory, and the observations cover a period

xiii

of some thirty years, — from the time when I first began to prowl about the home woods with a child's wonder and delight to my last hard winter trip into the Canadian wilderness. Some of the chapters, like those of the Woodcock and the Coon, represent the characteristics of scores of animals and birds of the same species; others, like those of the Bear and Eider-Duck in "Animal Surgery," represent the acute intelligence of certain individual animals that nature seems to have lifted enormously above the level of their fellows; and in a single case — that of the Toad — I have, for the story's sake, gathered into one creature the habits of four or five of these humble little helpers of ours that I have watched at different times and in different places.

The queer names herein used for beasts and birds are those given by the Milicete Indians, and represent usually some sound or suggestion of the creatures themselves. Except where it is plainly stated otherwise, all the incidents and observations have passed under my own eyes and have been confirmed

later by other observers. In the records, while
holding closely to the facts, I have simply
tried to make all these animals as interesting
to the reader as they were to me when I
discovered them.

Preface

WM. J. LONG.

Stamford, September, 1903.

CONTENTS

xvii

Full Page Illustrations

THE POINT
OF VIEW

THE POINT OF VIEW

AN old Indian, whom I know well, told me that he once caught a bear in his deadfall. That same day the bear's mate came and tried to lift away the heavily weighted log that had fallen on her back and crushed her. Failing in this he broke his way into the inclosure; and when the Indian came, drawn in on silent, inquisitive feet by a curious low sound in the air, the bear was sitting beside his dead mate, holding her head in his arms, rocking it to and fro, moaning.—

Two things must be done by the modern nature writer who would first understand the animal world and then share his discovery with others. He must collect his facts, at first hand if possible, and then he must interpret the facts as they appeal to his own head and heart in the light of all the circumstances that surround them. The child will be content with his animal story, but the man will surely ask the why and the how of every fact of animal life that particularly appeals to him. For every fact is also a revelation, and is chiefly interesting, not for itself, but for the law or the life which lies behind it and which it in some way expresses. An apple falling to the ground was a common enough fact, — so common that it had no interest until some one thought about it and found the great law that grips alike the falling apple and the falling star.

It is so in the animal world. The common facts of color, size, and habit were seen for centuries, but had little meaning or interest until some one thought about them and

gave us the law of species.   For most birds
and animals these common facts and their
meaning are now well known, and it is a
wearisome and thankless task to go over
them again.   The origin of species and the
law of gravitation are now put in the same
comfortable category with the steam engine
and the telegraph wire and other things that
we think we understand.   Meanwhile the air
has unseen currents that are ready to bear
our messages, and the sun wastes enough
energy on our unresponsive planet daily to
make all our fires unneces-
sary, if we but
understood.
Meanwhile, in

*The Point
of View*

the animal world, an immense array of new facts are hidden away, or are slowly coming to light as nature students follow the wild things in their native haunts and find how widely they differ one from another of the same kind, and how far they transcend the printed lists of habits that are supposed to belong to them.

We were too long content with the ugly telegraph pole and wire as the limit of perfection in communication; and we have been too well satisfied with the assumption that animals are governed by some queer, unknown thing called instinct, and that all are alike that belong to the same class. That is true only outwardly. It is enough to give the animal a specific name, but no more; and an animal's name or species is not the chief thing about him. You are not through with Indians when you have determined their race. That is sufficient for ethnology; to write in a book: possibly also the Calvinistic theologian was one time satisfied therewith; but the Indian's life still remains, more important than his race, and only after two centuries of neglect, or persecution, or injustice, are we awaking to the fact that his life is one of extraordinary human interest. His medicine lore and his thoughts of God lie deeper than the curve of his cranium; his legends and his rude music must be interpreted, as well as the color of his skin, and we are but just beginning to see the meaning of these larger things.

All this is only an analogy and proves nothing. However, it may suggest, if one thinks about it, that possibly we have made a slightly similar mistake about the animals; that we are not quite through with them when we have cried instinct and named their species, nor altogether justified in killing them industriously off the face of the earth—as we once did with the poor Beothuk Indians for the skins that they wore. Beneath their fur and feathers is their life; and a few observers are learning that their life also, with its faint suggestion of our own primeval childhood, is one of intense human interest. Some of them plan and calculate; and mathematics, however elementary, is hardly a matter of instinct. Some of them build dams and canals; some have definite social regulations; some rescue comrades; some bind their own wounds, and even set a broken leg, as will be seen in one of the following chapters. All higher orders communicate more or less with each other, and train their young, and modify their habits to meet changing conditions. These things, and many more quite as wonderful, are also facts. We are still waiting for the naturalist who will tell us truly what they mean.

I have had these two things — the new facts and the interpretation thereof — in mind in putting together the following sketches from my note-books and wilderness records. The facts have been carefully selected from many years' observations, with a view of emphasizing some of the unusual or unknown things of the animal world. Indeed, in all my work, or rather play, out of doors I have tried to discover the unusual things, — the things that mark an animal's individuality, — leaving the work of general habits and specific classification to other naturalists who know more and can do it better. Therefore have I passed over a hundred animals or birds to watch one, and have recorded only the rare observations, such as are seldom seen, and then only by men who spend long days and seasons in the woods in silent watchfulness.

Whether these rare habits are common property among the species, and seem strange to us only because we know so very little of the hidden life of wild animals, or whether they are the discovery of

The Point of View

a few rare individuals better endowed by nature than their fellows, I must leave to the reader to determine; for I do not know. This determination, however, must come, not by theory or prejudice or *a priori* reasoning, but simply by watching the animals more closely when they are unconscious of man's presence and so express themselves naturally. As a possible index in the matter I might suggest that I have rarely made an observation, however incredible it seemed to me at the time, without sooner or later finding some Indian or trapper or naturalist who had seen a similar thing among the wild creatures. The woodcock genius, whose story is recorded here, is a case in point. So is the porcupine that rolled down a long hill for the fun of the thing apparently — an observation that has been twice confirmed, once by a New Brunswick poacher and again by a Harvard instructor. So also are the wildcat that stole my net, and the heron that chummed little fish by a bait, and the fox that played possum when caught in a coop, and the kingfishers that stocked a pool with minnows for their little ones to catch, and the toad that learned to sit on a cow's hoof and wait for the flies at milking time. All these and a score more of incredible things, seen by different observers in different places, would seem to indicate that intelligence is more widely spread among the Wood Folk than we had supposed; and that, when we have opened our eyes wider and cast aside our prejudices, we shall learn that Nature is generous, even to the little folk, with her gifts and graces.

As for the interpretation of the facts, upon which I have occasionally ventured, — that is wholly my own and is of small consequence beside the other. Its value is a purely personal one, and I record it rather to set the reader thinking for himself than to answer his questions. In the heart of every man will be found the measure of his world, whether it be small or great. He will judge heat, not by mathematical computation of the sun's energy, but by the twitch of his burned finger, as every other child does; and comprehend the law of reaction, not from Ganot's treatise, but by pulling on his own boot-straps. So, with all the new facts of animal life before him, he will still live in a blind world and understand nothing until he have the courage to look in his own heart and read.

A Little Brother To The Bear

A Little Brother To The Bear

FEW knew the way to the little house in the rocks where the Little Brother to the Bear lived. It was miles away from every other house but one, in the heart of the big still woods. You had to leave the highway where it dipped into a cool dark hollow among the pines, and follow a lonely old road that the wood-choppers sometimes used in winter, and that led you, if you followed it far enough, to a tumble-down old mill on another cross-road, where the brook chattered and laughed all day long at the rusty wheel, and the phœbe built unmolested

15

under the sagging beams, and you could sometimes hear a trout jumping among the foam bubbles in the twilight. But you did not go so far if you wanted to find where the Little Brother to the Bear lived.

As you followed the wood road you came suddenly to a little clearing, with a brook and a wild meadow and a ledge all covered with ferns. The road twisted about here, as a road always does in going by a pretty place, as if it were turning back for another look. There was a little old house under the ledge wherein some shy, silent children lived; and this was the only dwelling of man on the three-mile road. Just beyond, at a point where the underbrush was thickest, an unnoticed cart path stole away from the wood road and brought you to a little pond in the big woods, at the spot where, centuries ago, the beavers had made a dam and a deep place for stowing their winter's wood. If you took a long pole and prodded deep in the mud here, you would sometimes find a cut stick of the beaver's food wood, its conical ends showing the strong tooth marks plainly, its bark still fresh and waiting to be eaten when the little owner should come back again; for that is what he cut it and put it there for, untold years ago. Very few ever thought of this, however; those who came to the spot had all their thoughts for the bullpouts that swarmed in the beaver's old storehouse and that would bite well on dark days. There were ledges all about the ancient dam and on both sides of the woodsy valley below; and among the mossy, fern-covered rocks of these ledges one of the shy children, with whom I had made friends, pointed out an arched doorway made by two great stones leaning against each other.

"Thome animal livth in there. I theen him. I peeked, one day, an' I theen hith eyeth wink; an', an', an' then I ran away," he said, his own eyes all round with the wonder of the woods.

We made no noise, but lay down under a bush together and watched the wonderful old doorway until it was time for the shy child to go home; but nothing came out, nor even showed a shining inquisitive eye in the doorway behind the screen of hanging ferns. Still we knew something was in there, for I showed my little woodsman, to his great wonder and delight, a short gray hair tipped with black clinging to the rocks. Then we went away more cautiously than we came.

"Maybe it's a coon," I told the shy child, "for they are sleepyheads and snooze all day. Foxy, too; they don't come out till dark and go in again before daylight, so that boys can't find out where they live."

When the time of full moon came I went back to the little house among the ledges, one afternoon, and hid under the same bush to watch until something should come out. But first I looked all about and found near by a huge hollow chestnut tree that the wood-choppers had passed by for years as not worth the cutting. There were scratches and claw pits everywhere in the rough bark, and just under the lower limbs was a big dark knot hole that might be a doorway to a den. So I lay down in hiding where I could see

both the tree and the fern-screened archway
among the rocks by simply turning my head.

At twilight there were sudden scratchings
in the hollow tree, mounting higher and
higher; then muffled grunts and whinings
and expostulations, as if little voices inside
the tree were saying: *My turn first. No,
mine! E-e-e-ahh, get out!* The whinings
stopped abruptly and a face appeared in the
dark knot hole — a sharp, pointed face with
alert ears and bright eyes that looked out
keenly over the still woods where only shadows were creeping about and only a wild
duck disturbed the silence, quacking softly
to her brood in the little pond. Then the
whining began again in the hollow tree, and
four other little faces pushed their sharp
noses into the knot hole, filling it completely,
all watching and listening, and wiggling their
chins down on their fellows' heads so as to
get a better view point, yet all eager as
children to be out and at play after their
long sleep.

One impatient little fellow clawed his way
upon his mother's back and thrust his face

out between her ears, and then I had a chance to see it better — a wonderful face, full of whims and drollery, with a white ring about its pointed muzzle, and a dark line running from the top of its nose and spreading into ebony rings around each eye, as if he were wearing queer smoked goggles, behind which the eyes twinkled and shone, or grew sober with much gravity as he heard the duck quacking. A keen face, yet very innocent, in which dog intelligence and fox cunning and bear drollery mingled perfectly; a face full of surprises, that set you smiling and think-ing at once; a fascinating, inquisitive face, the most lovable and contradictious among the Wood Folk, — the face of Mooweesuk the coon, the Little Brother to the Bear, as Indian and naturalist unite in calling him.

The mother came out first and sagged away backwards down the tree, swinging her head from side to side to look down and see how far yet, in true bear fashion. The four little ones followed her, clawing and whining their way to the bottom — all but one, who when half-way down turned and jumped,

"The little ones came out of their den
and began playing together"

landing on his mother's soft back to save himself trouble. Then she led the way to the doorway among the rocks, and the young followed in single file, winding about on her trail, stopping and sniffing when she did, and imitating her every action, just as young bear cubs do when roaming about the woods.

At the mouth of the den she stepped aside, and the young filed in out of sight one after another. The mother looked and listened for a moment, then scuttled away through the woods as a clear tremulous whinny came floating in through the twilight. A moment later I saw her on the shore of the pond with a larger coon, her mate probably, who had been asleep in another hollow tree by himself; and the two went off along the shore frogging and fishing together.

The mother had scarcely disappeared when the little ones came out of their den and began playing together, rolling and tumbling about like a litter of fox cubs, doing it for fun purely, yet exercising every claw and muscle for the hard work that a coon must do when he is called upon to take care of himself. After a time one of the cubs left his brothers playing and went back to the chestnut tree by the same way that he had come, following every turn and winding of the back trail as if there were a path there —as there probably was, to his eyes and nose, though mine could not find any. He climbed the tree as if he were after something, and disappeared into the knot hole, where I could hear the little fellow whining and scratching his way down inside the tree. In a moment he reappeared with something in his mouth. In the dusk I could not make out what it was, but as he came back and passed within ten feet of where I was hiding I had my field-glasses upon him and saw it plainly —a little knot of wood with a crook in it, the solitary plaything which you will find, all smooth from much handling, in almost every house where the Little Brother to the Bear has lived.

He carried it back to where the young coons were playing, lay down among them, and began to play by himself, passing the plaything back and forth through his wonderful front paws, striking it up, catching it, and rolling it around his neck and under his body, as a child does who has but one plaything. Some of the other coons joined him, and the little crooked knot went whirling back and forth between them, was rolled and caught, and hidden and found again, — all in silent intentness and with a pleasure that even in the twilight was unmistakable.

In the midst of this quiet play there came a faint ripple and splash of water, and the little coons dropped their plaything and stood listening, eyes all bright behind their dark goggles, noses wiggling, and ears cocked at the plashing on the pond shore. The mother was there diligently sousing something that she had caught; and presently she appeared and the little ones forgot their play in the joy of eating. But it was too far away and the shadows were now too dark to see what it was that she had brought home, and how she divided it among them. When she went away again it had grown dark enough for safety, and the young followed her in single file to the pond shore, where I soon lost them among the cool shadows.

That was the beginning of a long acquaintance, cultivated sometimes by day, more often by night; sometimes alone, when I would catch one of the family fishing or clamming or grubbing roots or nest robbing; sometimes with a boy, who caught two of the family in his traps; and again with the hunters under the September moon, when some foxy old coon would gather a freebooter band about him and lead them out to a raid on the cornfields. There each coon turned himself promptly into an agent of destruction and, reveling in the unwonted abundance, would pull down and destroy like a child savage, and taste twenty milky ears of corn before he found one that suited him perfectly; and then, too full for play or for roaming about to find all the hollow trees in the woods, he would take himself off to the nearest good den and sleep till he was hungry again and the low whinny of the old leader called him out for another raid.

Could we have followed the family on this first night of their wanderings, before the raids began and the dogs had scattered them, we would have understood why Mooweesuk is called a brother to the bear. Running he steps on his toes like a dog; and anatomically, especially in the development of the skull and ear bones, he suggests the prehistoric ancestor of both dog and wolf; but otherwise he is a pocket-edition of Mooween in all his habits. The mother always leads, like a bear, and the little ones follow in single file, noting everything that the mother calls attention to. They sit on their haunches and walk flat-footed, like a bear, leaving a track from their hind feet like that of a dwarf baby. Everything eatable in the woods ministers to their hunger, as it does to that of the greedy prowler in the black coat. Now they stir up an ant's nest; now they grub into a rotten log for worms and beetles. If they can find sweet sap, or a bit of molasses in an old camp, they dip their paws in it and then lick them clean, as Mooween does. They hunt now for wintergreen berries, and now for a woodmouse. They find a shallow place in the brook when the suckers are running and wait there till the big fish go by, when they

A Little Brother To The Bear

flip them out with their paws and scramble after them. From this fishing they turn to lush water-grass, or to digging frogs and turtles out of the mud; and the turtle's shell is cracked by dropping a stone upon it. Now they steal into the coop and scuttle away with a chicken; and after eating it they come back to the garden to crack a pumpkin open and make a dessert of the seeds. Now they see a muskrat swimming by in the pond with a mussel in his mouth, and they follow after him along the bank; for Musquash has a curious habit of eating in regular places — a flat rock, a stranded log, a certain tussock from which he has cut away the grass — and will often gather half a dozen or more clams and mussels before he sits down to dine. Mooweesuk watches till he finds the place; then, while Musquash is gone away after more clams, he will run off with all that he finds on the dining table. A score of times, on the ponds and streams, I have read the record of this little comedy. You can always

tell the place where Musquash eats by the pile of mussel shells in the water below it; and sometimes you will find Mooweesuk's track stealing down to the place, and if you follow it you will find where he cracked the clams that Musquash had gathered.

There is another way in which Mooweesuk is curiously like a bear: he wanders very widely, but he has regular beats, like Mooween, and if not disturbed always comes back with more or less regularity to any place where you have once seen him, and comes by the same unseen path. Like Mooween, his knowledge of the woods is wide and accurate. He knows — partly by searching them out, and partly from his mother, who takes him and shows him where they are — every den and hollow tree that will shelter a coon in times of trouble. He has always one den near a cornfield, where he can sleep when too full or too lazy to travel; he has one dry tree for stormy weather, and one cool mossy shell in deep shadow for the hot summer days. He has at least one sunny nook in the top of a hollow stub, where he loves to lie and soak

in the fall sunshine; and one favorite giant tree with the deepest and warmest hollow, which he invariably uses for his long winter sleep. And besides all these he has at least one tower of refuge near every path of his, to which he can betake himself when sudden danger threatens from dogs or men.

Though he walks and hunts and fights and feeds like a bear, Mooweesuk has many habits of his own that Mooween has never approached. One of these is his habit of nest robbing. Mooween does that, to be sure, for he is fond of eggs; but he must confine himself largely to ground-birds and to nests that he can reach by standing on his hind legs. Therefore are the woodpeckers all safe from him. Mooweesuk, on his part, can never see a hole in a tree without putting his nose into it to find out whether it contains any eggs or young woodpeckers. If it does contain them, he will reach a paw down, clinging close to the tree and stretching and pushing his arm into the hole clear to his shoulder, to see if perchance the nest be not a foolishly shallow one and the eggs lie within reach of his paw — which suggests a monkey's, by the way, in its handlike flexibility.

Once, on the edge of a wild orchard, I saw him rob a golden-winged woodpecker's nest in this way. The mother bird flew out as Moo-weesuk came scratching up the tree, which assured him that he would find something worth while within. He stretched in a paw, caught an egg, and appeared to be rolling it up, holding it against the side of the tunnel. When the egg was almost up to the entrance he put in his nose to see the treasure. Then it slipped and fell back, and probably broke. He tried another, got it up safely, and ate it whole where he was. He tried a third, which slipped and broke like the first. At this, with the taste of fresh egg in his mouth, he seemed to grow impatient, or perhaps he got an idea from the yellow streaks on his claws. He jabbed his paw down hard to break all the eggs, and drew it up dripping. He licked it clean with his tongue and put it back again into the yellow mess at the bottom. This was easy, and he kept it up until his moist paw brought up only shells and rotten wood,

when he backed away down the tree and shuffled off into the woods, leaving a sad mess for a mother woodpecker to face behind him.

Another habit in which he has improved upon Mooween is his fishing. He knows how to flip fish out of water with his paw, as all bears do; but he has also learned how to attract them when they are not to be found on the shallows. Many times in the twilight I have found Mooweesuk sitting very still on a rock or gray log beside the pond or river, his soft colors and his stillness making him seem like part of the shore. Other naturalists and hunters have mentioned the same thing, and their testimony generally agrees in this: that Mooweesuk's eyes are half shut at such times, and his sensitive feelers, or whiskers, are playing on the surface of the water. The fish below, seeing this slight motion but not seeing the animal above, attracted either by curiosity or, more likely, by the thought of insects playing, rise to the surface and are snapped out by a sweep of Mooweesuk's paw.

In a lecture, many years ago, Dr. Samuel Lockwood, a famous naturalist, first called attention to this curious way of angling. Since then I have many times seen Mooweesuk at his fishing; but I have never been fortunate enough to see him catch anything, though I have seen a wildcat do the trick perfectly in the same cunning way. Remembering his fondness for fish, and the many places where I have seen that he has eaten them and where the water was too deep to flip them out in the ordinary bear way, I have no doubt whatever that Dr. Lockwood has discovered the true secret of his patient waiting above the pools where the fish are feeding.

There is another curious habit of the coon which distinguishes him from the bear and from all other animals. That is, his habit of washing, or rather of sousing, everything he catches in water. No matter what he finds to eat, — mice, chickens, roots, grubs, fruit — everything, in fact, but fish, — he will take it to water, if he be anywhere near a pond or brook, and souse it thoroughly before eating.

Why he does this is largely a matter of guess-work. It is not to clean it, for much of it is already clean; not to soften it, for clams are soft enough as they are, and his jaws are powerful enough to crush the hardest shells, yet he souses them just the same before eating. Possibly it is to give things the watery taste of fish, of which he is very fond; more probably it is a relic, like the dog's turning around before he lies down, or like the unnecessary migration of most birds, the inheritance from some forgotten ancestor that had a reason for the habit, and that lived on the earth long, long years before there was any man to watch him or to wonder why he did it.

Deep in the wilderness Mooweesuk is shy and alert for danger, like most of the wild things there; but if approached very quietly, or if he find you unexpectedly near him, he is filled with the Wood Folk's curiosity to know who you are. Once, on the long tote-road from St. Leonards to the headwaters of the Restigouche, I saw Mooweesuk sitting on a rock by a trout brook diligently sousing something that he had just caught. I crept near on all fours to the edge of an old bridge, when the logs creaked under my weight and he looked up from his washing and saw me. He left his catch on the instant and came up the brook, part wading, part swimming, put his forepaws on the low bridge, poked his head up over the edge, and looked at me steadily, his face within ten feet of mine. He disappeared after a few moments and I crawled to the edge of the bridge to see what it was that he was washing. A faint scratching made me turn round, and there he was, his paws up on the other edge of the bridge, looking back at the queer man-thing that he had never seen before. He had passed under the bridge to look at me from the other side, as a fox invariably does if you keep still enough. The game that he was washing was a big frog, and after a few moments he circled the bridge, grabbed his catch, and disappeared into the woods.

Near towns where he is much hunted Mooweesuk has grown wilder, like the fox, and learned a hundred tricks that formerly

he knew nothing about. Yet even here, if found young, he shows a strange fearlessness and even a rare confidence in man. Once, in the early summer, I found a young coon at the foot of a ledge, looking up at a shelf a few feet above his head and whimpering because he could not get up. It was a surprise to him, evidently, that his claws could not make the same impression on the hard rock that they did on the home tree in which he was born. He made no objection — indeed, he seemed to take it as the most natural thing in the world — when I picked him up and put him on the shelf that he was whimpering about; but in a moment, like a baby, he wanted to get down again, and again I ministered to his necessities. When I went away he followed after me whimpering, forgetting his own den and his fellows in the ledge hard by, and was not satisfied till I took him up, when he curled down in the hollow of my arm and went to sleep perfectly contented.

Presently he waked up, cocking his ears and twisting his head dog fashion at some sound that was too faint for my ears, and poked his inquisitive nose all over me, even putting it down inside my collar, where it felt like a bit of ice creeping about my neck. Not till he had clawed his way inside my coat and put his nose in my vest pocket did he find the cause of the mysterious sounds which he heard. It was my watch ticking, and in a moment he had taken it out and was playing with the bright thing, as pleased as a child with a new plaything. He made a famous pet, full of tricks and drollery, catching chickens by pretending to be asleep when they came stretching their necks for the crumbs in his dish, playing possum when he was caught in mischief, drinking out of a bottle, full of joy when he could follow the boys to the woods, where he ran wild with delight but followed them home at twilight, and at last going off by himself to his home tree to sleep away the winter — but I must tell about all that elsewhere.

Like the bear, Mooweesuk is a peaceable fellow and tends strictly to his own affairs as he wanders wide through the woods.

This is not from fear, for no animal, except perhaps the wolverine — who is a terrible beast — is more careless of danger or faces it with such coolness and courage when it appears. Of a dog or two he takes little heed. If he hear them on his trail, he generally climbs a tree to get out of the way; for your dog, unlike his wild brother, the wolf, is a meddlesome fellow and must needs be worrying everything; and Mooweesuk, like most other wild creatures, loves peace, hunts only when hungry, and would always prefer to avoid a row if possible. When caught on the ground, or cornered, or roused to action by a sudden attack, he backs up against the nearest tree or stone to keep his enemies from getting at him from behind, and then fights till he is dead or till none of his enemies are left to bother him, when he goes quietly on his way again. No matter how great the odds or how terribly he is punished, I have never seen a coon lose his nerve or turn his back to run away. If the dogs be many and he is near a pond or river, he will lead them into deep water, where he is at

home, and then swimming rapidly in circles will close with them one by one and put them out of the fight most effectively. His method here seldom varies. He will whirl in suddenly on the dog that he has singled out, grip him about the neck with one arm, saw away at his head with his powerful teeth, at the same time slashing him across the eyes with his free claws, and then pile his weight on the dog's head to sink him under and drown all the rest of the fight out of him. That is generally enough for one dog; and Mooweesuk, without a scratch and with his temper cool as ice, will whirl like a flash upon his next victim.

Fortunately such troublous times are rare in Mooweesuk's life, and the wilderness coon knows little about them. His life from beginning to end is generally a peaceable one, full of good things to eat, and of sleep and play and a growing knowledge of the woods. He is born in the spring, a wee, blind, hairless little fellow, like a mole or a bear cub. As he grows he climbs to the entrance to his den, and will sit there as at a window for hours at a time, just his nose and eye visible, looking out on the new, bright, rustling world of woods, and blinking sleepily in the flickering sunshine. Then come the long excursions with his mother, at first by day when savage beasts are quiet, then at twilight, and then at last the long night rambles, in which, following his leader, he learns a hundred things that a coon must know: to follow the same paths till he comprehends the woods; to poke his inquisitive nose into every crack and cranny, for the best morsels on his bill of fare hide themselves in such places; to sleep for a little nap when he is tired, resting on his forehead so as to hide his brightly marked face and make himself inconspicuous, like a rock or a lichen-covered stump; to leap down from the tallest tree without hurting himself; and when he uses a den in the earth or rocks, to have an exit some distance away from the entrance, and never under any circumstances to enter his den save by his front door. There is great wisdom in this last teaching. When a dog finds a hole with a trail that always leads out of it he goes away, knowing it is of no use to bark there; but when he finds an opening into which a trail is leading, he thinks of course that his game is inside, and proceeds to howl and to dig without ever a thought in his foolish head that there may be another way out. Meanwhile, as he digs and raises an unpardonable row in the quiet woods, Mooweesuk will either wait just inside the entrance till she gets a chance to nip the dog's nose or crush his paw, or else will slip quietly out of the back door with her little ones and take them off to a hollow tree where they can sleep in peace and have no fear till the dog goes away.

By the time the first snows blow the little coons are well grown and strong enough to take good care of themselves; and then, like the bear again, they escape the cold and the hunger of winter by going to sleep for four or five months in a warm den that they have selected carefully during their summer wanderings. They are fat as butter when they curl themselves up for their long sleep; their ringed tails cover their sensitive noses, and if they waken for a time they suck their paws drowsily till they sleep again, so that, like the bear, they are often tender-footed when they come out in the spring.

Often the young coons of the same family sleep all together in the same den. The old males prefer to den by themselves, and are easily found; but the mother coon, like the mother bear, takes infinite pains to hide herself away where she can bring forth her young in peace, and where no one will ever find them.

There is one curious habit suggested by these winter dens that I have never seen explained, and for which I cannot account satisfactorily. On certain soft days in winter Mooweesuk wakes from his long sleep and wanders off into the world. At times you may follow his track for miles through the woods without finding that he goes anywhere or does anything in particular, for I have never found that he has eaten anything on these wanderings. Sometimes, miles away from his den, his track turns aside and goes straight to a hollow tree where other coons are spending the winter. It may possibly be that they are his own family, who generally have a den of their own, and whom he visits to see if all is well. Sometimes from this den another coon goes out with him, and their tracks wander for miles together; more often he comes out alone, and you follow to where he has visited other coons, or gone to sleep in another tree of his own, or swung round in a vast circle to the tree from which he started, where he goes to sleep again till called out for another season by the spring sun and the chickadee's love notes.

It may be that all this is a bit of pure sociability on Mooweesuk's part, for it is certainly not his season of love-making or of finding a mate. Often, as I have said, three or four cubs will sleep the winter out in the same den; but again you may find two or three old coons in the same tree. Unlike many other animals with regard to their dens, the law of hospitality is strong with the coon, and a solitary old fellow that prefers to den by himself will never refuse to share his winter house with other coons that

are driven out of their snug shelter; and this holds true notwithstanding the fact that there are plenty other hollow trees that seem to belong to the tribe in general, for they are visited freely by every passing coon.

There is another way in which this love of his race is manifest, and it brings a thrill of admiration for Mooweesuk whenever it is seen: he always comes in the face of danger or death to the cry of distress from one of his own kind. I have seen this several times, and once when it gave a thrill to the wild sport of night hunting that had unexpected consequences. It was near midnight in late November, at the end of the hunting season. The dogs had treed a coon, and by the aid of a bright fire of crackling brush we were trying to "shine his eye," that is, to locate the game in the tree-tops by the fierce glow of his eyes flashing back the firelight. We saw it at last, and one of the hunters climbed the tree and tried to poke the coon from his perch with a stout pole. Instead of doing as was expected of him, Mooweesuk, who is always cool in the face of any danger, came

"Leaping out of the tree-top and hurling
himself into the fight"

swiftly along the limb showing his teeth, and
with a snarl in his nose that was unmistakable. The hunter dropped his pole, pulled a
revolver from his pocket and shot the coon,
which in a sudden rage turned and leaped for
the howling dogs forty feet below. In a flash
there was a terrible fight on. Mooweesuk,
backed up against a tree, began the cool
swift snaps and blows that took all the courage out of half his enemies. Now a dog was
disabled by a single wolf grip on his sensitive
nose; now a favorite drew back howling, half-
blinded by a lightning sweep of Mooweesuk's
paw across both eyes. But the dogs were
too many for any one fighter however brave.
They leaped in upon Mooweesuk from the
sides; two powerful dogs stretched him out;
then, knowing that his fight was almost lost,
he twisted his head and gave a sudden fierce
cry, the help call, entirely different from his
screech and snarl of battle. Like a flash
another coon, a young one, appeared on the
scene, leaping out of the tree-top and hurling
himself into the fight, clawing and snapping
like a fury, and sending out his battle yell.

Up to that moment none of us had suspected that there was a second coon anywhere near. He had remained hidden and safe in the tree-top through all the uproar, until what seemed plainly a call for help came, when he threw all thought of self aside and came down like a hero.

We had not half realized all this when the little fellow threw himself upon the dog that held the first coon's neck and crushed a paw with a single grip of his powerful jaws. Then the bigger coon was on his feet again fighting feebly. — But a curious change had come over the hunt. I had jumped forward to interfere at the unexpected heroism, but had drawn back at the thought that I was only a guest, and there by courtesy. Near me stood a big hunter, an owner of some of the dogs, whose face was twitching strangely in the firelight. He started for the fight swinging a club, then drew back ashamed to show any weak sentiment in a coon hunt. "Save him," I whispered in his ear, "the little fellow deserves his life"; and again he jumped forward. "Drag off the dogs!" he

roared in a terrible voice, at the same time
pulling away his own. Every hunter understood. There was a sudden wild yell with a
thrill in it that made one's spine tingle glori-
ously. The dogs were dragged away by tails
and legs, struggling and howling against the
indignity; the big coon lay down quietly to
die; but the little fellow put his back up
against a rock, his eyes glowing like coals
that the wind blows upon, wrinkled his
nose like a wolf, and snarled his defiance
at the whole howling mob. And there
he stayed till I took a pole and amid
laughs and cheers drove him, still protesting savagely, into another tree where
the dogs could not get at him.

That was far away from the place
where my first Little Brother to the Bear
lived, and many years had passed since
I had visited the ledge by the old beaver
dam. One day I came back, and turned
swiftly into the old wood road that had a
happy memory for me by every turn and
rock and moldering stump. Here was

where the grouse used to drum; and there, at the end of the log, were signs to tell me that it still sometimes rolled off the muffled thunder of the wings above. Here was the break in the wall that the fox used as a runway; and there was a crinkly yellow hair caught on a rough rock telling its story mutely. Here was where the pines stood thickest; but they were all cut away now, and the hardwood seeds that had waited so many years under the pines for their chance at the sunlight were shooting up into vigorous life at last. And here was the place where the road twisted about to look back on the pretty spot where the shy children lived, with whom I had once made friends.

They were all gone, and the little house under the ledge was deserted. In one of the tumble-down rooms I found a rag doll beside the cold hearth, and some poor toys on a shelf under a broken window. In the whole lonely forgotten house these were the only things that brought the light to one's face and the moisture to his eyes as he beheld them. All else spoke of ruin and decay; but these poor playthings that little hands had touched went straight to the heart with an eternal suggesting of life and innocence and a childhood that never grows old in the world. I dusted them tenderly with my handkerchief and put them back in their places, and went away softly down the path that led to the other house where the Little Brother to the Bear used to live.

Everything was changed here, too. The dam that the beavers had built, and that the years had covered over, still stood as strong as ever; but the woods had been cut away, and the pond had dwindled till the wild duck no longer found a refuge there. The ledges were no longer green, for the sun that came in when the big trees fell had killed most of the mosses and ferns that decked them; and the brook's song, though cheery still, was scarcely heard as it trickled and seeped where once it had rushed and tumbled down the woodsy valley, which remained woodsy still, because happily the soil there was too poor to raise anything but brush and cowslips, and so the woodsmen had spared it from desolation.

The old tree that had once been the coon's house was blown down. When it missed the support and the wind-break of its fellows, it could not stand alone, and toppled over in the first storm. The old claw marks of Moowee-suk were hidden deep under lichens. From this ruined home I went to the den among the rocks by the path that the coons used to follow. The hunters had been here long ago; the den was pried open, the sheltering rocks were thrust aside, and the interior was full of last year's leaves. As I brushed them away sadly to see what the house was like, my hand struck something hard in a dark corner, and I brought it out into the light again. It was a little knot with a crook in it, all worn smooth by much handling—the plaything that I had first seen, and that was now the last memory of a home where the Little Brothers to the Bear had once lived and played together happily.

WHITOOWEEK, THE HERMIT

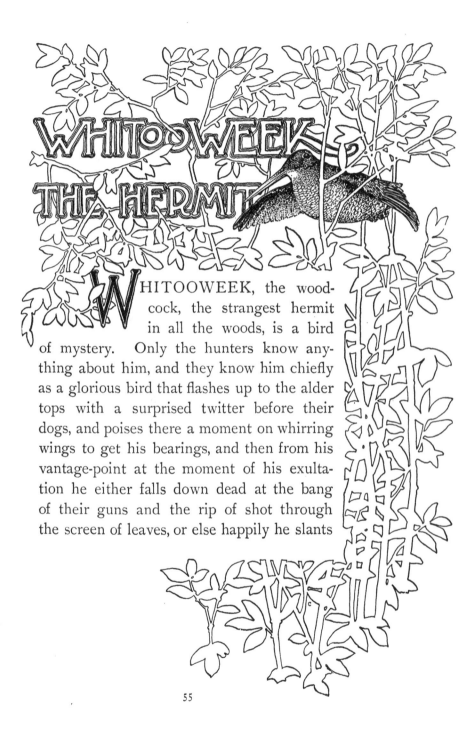

WHITOOWEEK THE HERMIT

WHITOOWEEK, the wood-
cock, the strangest hermit
in all the woods, is a bird
of mystery. Only the hunters know anything about him, and they know him chiefly
as a glorious bird that flashes up to the alder
tops with a surprised twitter before their
dogs, and poises there a moment on whirring
wings to get his bearings, and then from his
vantage-point at the moment of his exultation he either falls down dead at the bang
of their guns and the rip of shot through
the screen of leaves, or else happily he slants

swiftly down to another hiding-place among the alders. To the hunters, who are practically his only human acquaintances, he is a game bird pure and simple, and their interest is chiefly in his death. The details of his daily life he hides from them, and from all others, in the dark woods, where he spends all the sunny hours, and in the soft twilight when he stirs abroad, like an owl, after his long day's rest. Of a hundred farmers on whose lands I have found Whitooweek or the signs of his recent feeding, scarcely five knew from observation that such a bird existed, so well does he play the hermit under our very noses.

The reasons for this are many. By day he rests on the ground in some dark bit of cover, by a brown stump that exactly matches his feathers, or in a tangle of dead leaves and brakes where it is almost impossible to see him. At such times his strange fearlessness of man helps to hide him, for he will let you pass within a few feet of him without stirring. That is partly because he sees poorly by day and perhaps does not realize how near you are, and partly because he knows that his soft colors hide him so well amidst his surroundings that you cannot see him, however near you come. This confidence of his is well placed, for once I saw a man step over a brooding woodcock on her nest in the roots of an old stump without seeing her, and she never moved so much as the tip of her long bill as he passed. In the late twilight when woodcock first stir abroad you see only a shadow passing swiftly across a bit of clear sky as Whitooweek goes off to the meadow brook to feed, or hear a rustle in the alders as he turns the dead leaves over, and a faint *peeunk*, like the voice of a distant night-hawk, and then you catch a glimpse of a shadow that flits along the ground, or a weaving, batlike flutter of wings as you draw near to investigate. No wonder, under such circumstances, that Whitooweek passes all his summers and raises brood upon brood of downy invisible chicks in a farmer's wood lot without ever being found out or recognized.

My own acquaintance with Whitooweek

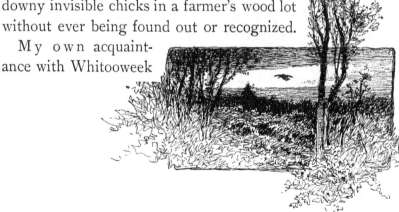

began when I was a child, when I had no name to give the strange bird that I watched day after day, and when those whom I asked for information laughed at my description and said no such bird existed. It was just beyond the upland pasture where the famous Old Beech Partridge lived. On the northern slopes were some dark, wet maple woods, and beyond that the ground slanted away through scrub and alders to a little wild meadow where cowslips grew beside the brook. One April day, in stealing through the maple woods, I stopped suddenly at seeing something shining like a jewel almost at my feet. It was an eye, a bird's eye; but it was some moments before I could realize that it was really a bird sitting there on her nest between the broken ends of an old stub that had fallen years ago.

I backed away quietly and knelt down to watch the queer find. Her bill was enormously long and straight, and her eyes were 'way up

at the back of her head — that was the first
observation. Some wandering horse had put
his hoof down and made a hollow in the
dry rotten wood of the fallen stub. Into
this hollow a few leaves and brown grass
stems had been gathered, — a careless kind
of nest, yet serving its purpose wonderfully,
for it hid the brooding mother so well that
one might step on her without ever knowing
that bird or nest was near. This was the
second wondering observation, as I made out
the soft outlines of the bird sitting there,
apparently without a thought of fear, within
ten feet of my face.

I went away quietly that day and left her
undisturbed; and I remember perfectly that
I took with me something of the wonder,
and something too of the fear, with which a
child naturally meets the wild things for the
first time. That she should be so still and
fearless before me was a perfect argument to
a child that she had some hidden means of
defense — the long bill, perhaps, or a hidden
sting — with which it was not well to trifle.
All that seems very strange and far away to

me now; but it was real enough then to a very small boy, alone in the dark woods, who met for the first time a large bird with an enormously long bill and eyes 'way up on the back of her head where they plainly did not belong, a bird moreover that had no fear and seemed perfectly well able to take care of herself. So I went away softly and wondered about it.

Next day I came back again. The strange bird was there on her nest as before, her long bill resting over the edge of the hollow and looking like a twig at the first glance. She showed no fear whatever, and encouraged at her quietness and assurance I crept nearer and nearer till I touched her bill with my finger and turned it gently aside. At this she wiggled it impatiently, and my first child's observation was one that has only recently been noticed by naturalists, namely, that the tip of the upper bill is flexible and can be moved about almost like the tip of a finger in order to find the food that lies deep in the mud, and seize it and drag it out of its hiding. At the same time she uttered a curious hissing sound that frightened me again and made me think of snakes and hidden stings; so I drew back and watched her from a safe distance. She sat for the most part perfectly motionless, the only movement being an occasional turning of the long bill; and once when she had been still a very long time, I turned her head aside again, and to my astonishment and delight she made no objection, but left her head as I had turned it, and presently she let me twist it back again. After her first warning she seemed to understand the situation perfectly, and had no concern for the wondering child that watched her and that had no intention whatever of harming her or her nest.

Others had laughed at my description of a brown bird with a long bill and eyes at the back of her head that let you touch her on her nest, so I said no more to them; but at the first opportunity I hunted up Natty Dingle and told him all about it. Natty was a gentle, harmless, improvident little man, who

Whitooweek
The Hermit

would never do any hard work for pay, — it gave him cricks in his back, he said, — but would cheerfully half kill himself to go fishing through the ice, or to oblige a neighbor. So far as he earned a living he did it by shooting and fishing and trapping and picking berries in their several seasons, and by gathering dandelions and cowslips (kewslops he called them) in the spring and peddling them good-naturedly from door to door. Most of his time in pleasant weather he spent in roaming about the woods, or lying on his back by the pond shore where the woods were thickest, fishing lazily and catching fish where no one else could ever get them, or watching an otter's den on a stream where no one else had seen an otter for forty years. He knew all about the woods, knew every bird and beast and plant, and one boy at least, to my knowledge, would rather go with him for a day's fishing than see the president's train or go to a circus.

Unlike the others, Natty did not laugh at my description, but listened patiently and told me I had found a woodcock's nest, — a rare thing, he said, for though he had roamed the woods so much, and shot hundreds of the birds in season, he had never yet chanced upon a nest. Next day he went with me, to see the eggs, he said; but, as I think of it now, it was probably with a view of locating the brood accurately for the August shooting. As we rounded the end of the fallen stub the woodcock's confidence deserted her at sight of the stranger, and she slipped away noiselessly into the leafy shadows. Then we saw her four eggs, very big at one end, very little at the other, and beautifully colored and spotted.

Natty, who was wise in his way, merely glanced at the nest and then drew me aside into hiding, and before we knew it, or had even seen her approach, Mother Woodcock was brooding her eggs again. Then Natty, who had doubted one part of my story, whispered to me to go out; and the bird never stirred as I crept near on hands and knees and touched her as before.

A few minutes later we crept away softly, and Natty took me to the swamp to show me the borings, telling me on the way of the woodcock's habits as he had seen them in the fall hunting. The borings we found in plenty wherever the earth was soft, — numerous holes, as if made with a pencil, where the woodcock had probed the earth with her long bill. She was hunting for earthworms, Natty told me, — a queer mistake of his, and of all the bird books as well, for in the primitive alder woods and swamps where the borings are so often seen, there are no earthworms, but only slugs and soft beetles and delicate white grubs. Woodcock hunt by scent and feeling, and also by listening for the slight sounds made by the worms underground, he told me, and that is why the eyes are far back on the head, to be out of the way, and also to watch for danger above and behind while the bird's bill is deep in the mud. And that also explains why the tip of the bill is flexible, so that when the bird bores in the earth and has failed to locate the game accurately by hearing, the sensitive tip of the bill feels around, like a finger, until it finds and seizes the morsel. All this and many things more he told me as we searched through the swamp for the signs of Mother Woodcock's hunting and made our way home together in the twilight. Some things were true, some erroneous; and some were a curious blending of accurate traditions and imaginative folk-lore from some unknown source, such as is still held as knowledge of birds and beasts in all country places; and these were the most interesting of all to a child. And the boy listened, as a devotee listens to a great sacred concert, and remembered all these things and afterwards sifted them and found out for himself what things were true.

When I went back to the spot, a few days later, the nest was deserted. A few bits of

shell scattered about told me the story, and
that I must now hunt for the little woodcocks, which are almost impossible to find
unless the mother herself show you where
they are. A week later, as I prowled along
the edge of the swamp, a sudden little brown
whirlwind seemed to roll up the leaves at
my feet. In the midst of it I made out
the woodcock fluttering away, clucking, and
trailing now a wing and now a leg, as if desperately hurt. Of course I followed her to
see what was the matter, forgetting the partridge that had once played me the same
pretty trick to decoy me away from her
chicks. When she had led me to a safe
distance all her injuries vanished as at the
touch of magic. She sprang up on strong
wings, whirled across the swamp
and circled swiftly back
to where I had first

started her. But I did not find one of the little woodcocks, though I hunted for them half an hour, and there were four of them, probably, hiding among the leaves and grass stems under my very eyes.

The wonderful knowledge gleaned from Natty Dingle's store and from the borings in the swamp brought me into trouble and conflict a few weeks later. Not far from me lived a neighbor's boy, a budding natu-ralist, who had a big yellow cat named Blink at his house. A queer old cat was Blink, and the greatest hunter I ever saw. He knew, for instance, where a mole could be found in his long tunnel, — and that is some-thing that still puzzles me, — and caught scores of them; but, like most cats, he could never be induced to taste one. When he caught a mole and was hungry, he would hide it and go off to catch a mouse or a bird; and these he would eat, leaving the mole to be brought home as game. He would hunt by himself for hours at a time, and come meowing home, bringing every-thing he caught, — rats, squirrels, rabbits, quail, grouse, and even grasshoppers when no bigger game was afoot. At a distance we would hear his call, a peculiar *yeow-yow* that he gave only when he had caught something, and the boy would run out to meet him and take his game, while Blink purred and rubbed against his legs to show his pride and satisfaction. When no one met him he would go meowing round the house once or twice and then put his game under the door-step, where our noses must speedily call it to our attention, for Blink would never touch it again.

One day the boy found a strange bird under the door-step, a beautiful brown creature, as large as a pigeon, with a long, straight bill, and eyes at the top of its head. He took it to his father, a dogmatic man, who gave him a queer mixture of truth and nonsense as his portion of natural history. It was a blind snipe, he said; and there was some truth in that. It could n't see because its eyes were out of place; it was a very

scarce bird that appeared occasionally in the
fall, and that burrowed in the mud for the
winter instead of migrating, — and all this
was chiefly nonsense.

When the boy took me to see his queer
find I called it a woodcock and began to tell
about it eagerly, but was stopped short and
called a liar for my pains. A wordy war
followed, in which Natty Dingle's authority
was invoked in vain; and the boy, being
bigger than I and in his own yard, drove me
away at last for daring to tell him about a
bird that his own cat had caught and that
his own father had called a blind snipe. He
pegged one extra stone after me for saying
that there were plenty of them about, only
they fed by night like owls, and another
stone for shouting back that they did not
burrow in the mud like turtles in dry weather,
as his oracle had declared. And this untem-
pered zeal is very much like what one generally encounters when he runs up against the
prejudices of naturalists anywhere. Hear
all they say, — that the earth is flat, that
swallows spend the winter in the mud, that

animals are governed wholly by instinct, — but don't quote any facts you may have seen until the world is ready for them. For it is better to call a thing a blind snipe, and know better, than to raise a family row and be hit on the head with a stone for calling it a woodcock.

The little woodcocks, though scarcely bigger than bumblebees, run about hardily, like young partridges, the moment they chip the shell, and begin at once to learn from the mother where to look for food. In the early twilight, when they are less wild and the mother is not so quick to flutter away and draw you after her, I have sometimes surprised a brood of them, — wee, downy, invisible things, each with a comically long bill and a stripe down his back that seems to divide the little fellow and hide one half of him even after you have discovered the other. The mother is with them, and leads them swiftly among the bogs and ferns and alder stems, where they go about turning over the dead leaves and twigs and shreds of wet bark with their bills for the grubs that hide

beneath, like a family of rag-pickers each with
a little stick to turn things over. Mother
and chicks have a contented little twitter at
such times that I have never heard under
any other circumstances, which is probably
intended to encourage each other and keep
all the family within hearing as they run
about in the twilight.

   When the feeding-grounds are far away
from the nest, as is often the case, Whitooweek has two habits that are not found, I
think, in any other game birds — except perhaps the plover; and I have never been able
to watch the young of these birds, though
every new observation of the old ones serves
to convince me that they are the most remarkable birds that visit us, and the least understood. When food must be hunted
for at a long distance, the mother
will leave her brood in hiding and
go herself to fetch it. When she
returns she feeds the chicks, like
a mother dove, by putting her bill
in their throats and giving each
his portion, going and coming

until they are satisfied, when she leaves them in hiding again and feeds for herself during the rest of the night. Like most other young birds and animals when left thus by their mothers, they never leave the spot where they have been told to stay, and can hardly be driven away from it until the mother returns. And generally, when you find a brood of young woodcock without the mother, they will let you pick them up and will lie as if dead in your hand, playing possum, until you put them down again.

When there is a good feeding-ground near at hand, yet too far for the little chicks to travel, the mother will take them there, one by one, and hide them in a secret spot until she has brought the whole family. Two or three times I have seen woodcock fly away with their young; and once I saw a mother return to the spot from which, a few moments before, she had flown away with a chick and take another from under a leaf where I had not seen him. This curious method is used by the mothers not only to take the young to favorable feeding-grounds, but also to get them quickly out of the way when sudden danger threatens, like fire or flood, from which it is impossible to hide.

Whitooweek
The Hermit

So far as I can judge the process, which is always quickly done and extremely difficult to follow, the mother lights or walks directly over the chick and holds him between her knees as she flies. This is the way it seems to me after seeing it several times. There are those — and they are hunters and keen observers — who claim that the mother carries them in her bill, as a cat carries a kitten; but how that is possible without choking the little fellows is to me incomprehensible. The bill is not strong enough at the tip, I think, to hold them by a wing; and to grasp them by the neck, as in a pair of shears, and so to carry them, would, it seems to me, most certainly suffocate or injure them in any prolonged flight; and that is not the way in which wild mothers generally handle their little ones.

There is another possible way in which Whitooweek may carry her young, though I have never seen it. An old hunter and keen

observer of wild life, with whom I sometimes roam the woods, once stumbled upon
a mother woodcock and her brood by a little
brook at the foot of a wild hillside. One of
the chicks was resting upon the mother's
back, just as one often sees a domestic
chicken. At my friend's sudden approach
the mother rose, taking the chick with her
on her back, and vanished among the thick
leaves. The rest of the brood, three of them,
disappeared instantly; and the man, after finding one of them, went on his way without
waiting to see whether the mother returned
for the rest. I give the incident for what it
is worth as a possible suggestion as to the
way in which young woodcock are carried to
and fro; but I am quite sure that those that
have come under my own observation were
carried by an entirely different method.

The young woodcock begin to use their
tiny wings within a few days of leaving the
eggs, earlier even than young quail, and fly
in a remarkably short time. They grow with
astonishing rapidity, thanks to their good
feeding, so that often by early summer the

" One of the chicks was resting
upon the mother's back "

family scatters, each one to take care of himself, leaving the mother free to raise another brood. At such times they travel widely in search of favorite food and come often into the farm-yards, spending half the night about the drains and stables while the house is still, and vanishing quickly at the first alarm; so that Whitooweek is frequently a regular visitor in places where he is never seen or suspected.

In his fondness for earthworms Whitooweek long ago learned some things that a man goes all his life without discovering, namely, that it is much easier and simpler to pick up worms than to dig for them. When a boy has to dig bait, as the price of going fishing with his elders, he will often spend half a day, in dry weather, working hard with very small results; for the worms are deep in the earth at such times and can be found only in favored places. Meanwhile the father, who has sent his boy out to dig, will spend a pleasant hour after supper in watering his green lawn. The worms begin to work their way up to the surface at the first patter of water-drops, and by midnight are crawling about the lawn by hundreds, big, firm-bodied fellows, just right for trout fishing. They stay on the surface most of the night; and that is why the early bird *catches* the worm, instead of digging him out, as the sleepy fellows must do. Midnight is the best time to go out with your lantern and get all the bait you want without trouble or worry. That is also the time when you are most likely to find Whitooweek at the same occupation. Last summer I flushed two woodcock from my neighbor's lawn in the late evening; and hardly a summer goes by that you do not read with wonder of their being found within the limits of a great city like New York, whither they have come from a distance by night to hunt the rich lawns over. For the same fare of earthworms they visit the gardens as well; and often in a locality where no woodcock are supposed to exist you will find, under the cabbage leaves, or in the cool shade of the thick corn-field, the round holes where Whitooweek has been probing the soft earth for grubs and worms while you slept.

When midsummer arrives a curious change comes over Whitooweek; the slight family ties are broken, and the bird becomes a hermit indeed for the rest of the year. He lives entirely alone, and not even in the migrating season does he join with his fellows in any large numbers, as most other birds do; and no one, so far as I know, has ever seen anything that might be appropriately called a flock of woodcock. The only exception to this rule that I know is when, on rare occasions, you surprise a male woodcock strutting on a log, like a grouse, spreading wings and tail, and hissing and sputtering queerly as he moves up and down. Then, if you creep near, you will flush two or three other birds that are watching beside the log, or in the underbrush close at hand. One hunter told me recently that his setter once pointed a bird on a fallen log, that ceased his strutting as soon as he was discovered and slipped down into the ferns. When the dog drew nearer, five woodcock flushed at the same moment, the greatest number that I have ever known being found together.

When I asked the unlearned hunter — who was yet wise in the ways of the woods — the reason for Whitooweek's strutting at this season, after the families have scattered, he had no theory or explanation. "Just a queer streak, same's most birds have, on'y queerer," he said, and let it go at that. I have seen the habit but once, and then imperfectly, for I blundered upon two or three birds and flushed them before I could watch the performance. It is certainly not to win his mate, for the season for that is long past; and unless it be a suggestion of the grouse habit of gathering in small bands for a kind of rude dance, I am at a loss to account for it. Possibly play may appeal even to Whitooweek, as it certainly appeals to all other birds; and it is play alone that can make him forget he is a hermit.

With the beginning of the molt the birds desert the woods and swamps where they were reared and disappear absolutely.

Whither they go at this time is a profound mystery.   In places where there were a dozen birds yesterday there are none to-day; and when you do stumble upon one it is generally in a spot where you never found one before, and where you will probably not find another, though you haunt the spot for years.   This is the more remarkable in view of the fact that the woodcock, like most other birds, has certain favored spots to which he returns, to nest or feed or sleep, year after year.

Occasionally at this season you may find a solitary bird on a dry southern hillside, or on the sunny edge of the big woods.   He is pitiful now to behold, having scarcely any feathers left to cover him, and can only flutter or run away at your approach.   If you have the rare fortune to surprise him now when he does not see you, you will note a curious thing.   He stands beside a stump or brake where the sun can strike his bare back fairly, as if he were warming himself at nature's fireplace. His

Whitooweek
The Hermit

Whitooweek
The Hermit

long bill rests its tip on the ground, as if it were a prop supporting his head. He is asleep; but if you crawl near and bring your glasses to bear, you will find that he sleeps with half an eye open. The lower lid seems to be raised till it covers half the eye; but the upper half is clear, so that as he sleeps he can watch above and behind for his enemies. He gives out very little scent at such times, and your keen-nosed dog, that would wind him at a stone's throw in the autumn, will now pass close by without noticing him, and must almost run over the bird before he draws to a point or shows any signs that game is near.

Hunters say that these scattered birds are
those that have lost the most feathers, and
that they keep to the sunny open spots for
the sake of getting warm. Perhaps they are
right; but one must still ask the question,
what do these same birds do at night when
the air is colder than by day? And, as if to
contradict the theory, when you have found
one bird on a sunny open hillside, you will
find the next one a mile away asleep in the
heart of a big corn-field, where the sun barely
touches him the whole day long.

Whatever the reason for their action, these
birds that you discover in July are rare, incomprehensible individuals. The bulk of
the birds disappear, and you cannot find
them. Whether they scatter widely to dense
hiding-places and by sitting close escape discovery, or whether, like some of the snipe,
they make a short northern migration in the
molting season in search of solitude and a
change of food, is yet to be discovered. For
it is astonishing how very little we know of
a bird that nests in our cow pasture and that
often visits our yards and lawns nightly, but

whose acquaintance we make only when he is dead and served as a delicious morsel, hot on toast, on our dining-tables.

In the spring, while winning his mate, Whitooweek has one habit which, when seen at the edge of the alder patch, reminds you instantly of the grass-plovers of the open moors and uplands, and of their wilder namesakes of the Labrador barrens. Indeed, in his fondness for burned plains, where he can hide in plain sight and catch no end of grasshoppers and crickets without trouble to vary

his diet, and in a swift changeableness and fearlessness of man, Whitooweek has many points in common with the almost unknown plovers. In the dusk of the evening, as you steal along the edge of the woods, you will hear a faint *peenk*,

peenk close beside you, and as you turn to listen and locate the sound a woodcock slants swiftly up over your head and begins to whirl in a spiral towards the heavens, clucking and twittering ecstatically. It is a poor kind of song, not to be compared with that of the oven-bird or grass-plover, who do the same thing at twilight, and Whitooweek must help his voice by the clicking of his wings and by the humming of air through them, like the sharp voice of a reed in windy weather; but it sounds sweet enough, no doubt, to the little brown mate who is standing perfectly still near you, watching and listening to the performance. At an enormous height, for him, Whitooweek whirls about madly for a few moments and then retraces his spiral downwards, clucking and twittering the while, until he reaches the tree-tops, where he folds his wings directly over his mate and drops like a plummet at her head. Still she does not move, knowing well what is coming, and when within a few feet of the ground Whit-ooweek spreads his wings wide to break his fall and drops quietly close beside her. There

Whitooweek
The Hermit

he remains quite still for a moment, as if exhausted; but the next moment he is strutting about her, spreading wings and tail like a wild turkey-gobbler, showing all his good points to the best advantage, and vain of all his performances as a peacock in the spring sunshine. Again he is quiet; a faint *peent, peent* sounds, as if it were a mile away; and again Whitooweek slants up on swift wings to repeat his ecstatic evolutions.

Both birds are strangely fearless of men at such times; and if you keep still, or move very softly if you move at all, they pay no more attention to you than if you were one of the cattle cropping the first bits of grass close at hand. Like the golden plover, whose life is spent mostly in the vast solitudes of Labrador and Patagonia, and whose nature is a curious mixture of extreme wildness and dense stupidity, they seem to have no instinctive fear of any large animal; and whatever fear Whitooweek has learned is the result of persistent hunting. Even in this he is slower to learn than any other game bird, and when let alone for a little season promptly returns to his native confidence.

When the autumn comes you will notice another suggestion of the unknown plover in Whitooweek. Just as you look confidently for the plover's arrival in the first heavy northeaster after August 20, so the first autumn moon that is obscured by heavy fog will surely bring the woodcock back to his accustomed haunts again. But why he should wait for a full moon, and then for a chill mist to cover it, before beginning his southern flight is one of the mysteries. Unlike the plovers that come by hundreds, and whose eerie cry, shrilling above the roar of the storm and the rush of rain, brings you out of your bed at midnight to thrill and listen and thrill again, Whitooweek slips in silent and solitary; and you go out in the morning, as to an appointment, and find him sleeping quietly just where you expected him to be.

With the first autumn flight another curious habit comes out, namely, that Whitooweek has a fondness for certain spots, not for any food or protection they give him, but evidently from long association, as a child loves certain unkempt corners of an upland pasture above twenty other more beautiful spots that one would expect him to like better. Moreover, the scattered birds, in some unknown way, seem to keep account of the place, as if it were an inn, and so long as they remain in the neighborhood will often keep this one particular spot filled to its full complement.

Some three miles north of where I write there is a certain small patch of tall open woods that a few hunters have known and tended for years, while others passed by carelessly, for it is the least likely looking spot for game in the whole region. Yet if there is but a single woodcock in all Fairfield County, in these days of many hunters and few birds, the chances are that he will be there; and if you do not find one there on the first morning after a promising spell of weather, you may be almost certain that the flight is not yet on, or has passed you by. Several times after flushing a solitary woodcock in

this spot I have gone over the whole place
to find some reason for Whitooweek's strange
fancy; but all in vain. The ground is open
and stony, with hardly a fern or root or
grass tuft to shelter even a woodcock; and
look as closely as you will you can find
no boring or sign of Whitooweek's feeding.
From all external appearances it is the last
spot where you would expect to find such a
bird, and there are excellent covers close at
hand; yet here is where Whitooweek loves
to lie during the day, and to this spot he
will return as long as there are any woodcock left. Hunters may harry the spot to-
day and kill the few rare birds that still visit
it; but to-morrow, if there be any birds in
the whole neighborhood, there will be practically the same number just where the first
were killed.

I have questioned old gunners about this
spot, — which I discovered by flushing two
woodcock at a time when none were to be
found, though they were searched for by a
score of young hunters and dogs, — and find
that it has been just so as long

as they can remember. Years ago, when the birds were plenty and little known, five or six might be found here on a half-acre at any time during the flight. If these were killed off, others took their places, and the supply seemed to be almost a constant quantity as long as there were birds enough in the surrounding coverts to draw upon; but why they haunt this spot more than others, and why the vacant places are so quickly filled, are two questions that no man can answer.

One hunter suggests to me, doubtfully, that possibly this may be accounted for by the migrating birds that are moving southward during the flight, and that drop into the best unoccupied places; and the same explanation will occur to others. The objection to this is that the birds migrate by night, and by night this spot is always unoccupied. The woodcock use it for a resting-place only by day, and by night they scatter widely to the feeding-grounds, whither also the migrating birds first make their way; for Whitooweek must feed often, his food being easily digested, and can probably make no sustained flights. He seems to move southward by easy stages, feeding as he goes; and so the new-comers would meet the birds that lately occupied the spot on the feeding-grounds, if indeed they met them at all, and from there would come with them at daylight to the resting-places they had selected. But how do the new-comers, who come by night, learn that the favored spots are already engaged by day, or that some of the birds that occupied them yesterday are now dead and their places vacant?

The only possible explanation is either to say that it is a matter of chance — which is no explanation at all, and foolish also; for chance, if indeed there be any such blind unreasonable thing in a reasonable world, does not repeat itself regularly — or to say frankly that there is some definite understanding and communication among the birds as they flit to and fro in the night; which is probably true, but obviously impossible to prove with our present limited knowledge.

This fondness for certain spots shows itself in another way when you are on the trail of the hermit. When flushed from a favorite resting-place and not shot at, he makes but a short flight, up to the brush tops and back again, and then goes quietly back to the spot from which he rose as soon as you are gone away. He has also the hare trick of returning in a circle to his starting-point; and occasionally, when you flush a bird and watch sharply, you may see him slant down on silent wings behind you and light almost at your heels. Once my old dog Don started a woodcock and remained stanchly pointing at the spot where he had been. I remained where I was, a few yards in the rear, and in a moment Whitooweek whirled in from behind and dropped silently into some brakes between me and the dog and not ten feet from the old setter's tail. The ruse succeeded perfectly, for as the scent faded away from Don's nose he went forward, and so missed the bird that was watching him close behind. This curious habit may be simply the result of Whitooweek's fondness for

"Once my old dog Don started
a woodcock"

certain places; or it may be that by night he carefully selects the spot where he can rest and hide during the day, and returns to it because he cannot find another so good while the sun dazzles his eyes; or it may be a trick pure and simple to deceive the animal that disturbs him, by lighting close behind where neither dog nor man will ever think of looking for him.

By night, when he sees perfectly and moves about rapidly from one feeding-ground to another, Whitooweek is easily dazzled by a light of any kind, and he is one of the many creatures that come and go within the circle of your jack. Because he is silent at such times, and moves swiftly, he is generally unnamed — just a night bird, you think, and let him pass without another thought. Several times when jacking, to see what birds and animals I might surprise and watch by night, I have recognized Whitooweek whirling wildly about my circle of light. Once, deep in the New Brunswick wilderness, I surprised two poachers spearing salmon at midnight with a fire-basket hung over the bow of their canoe. Spite of its bad name it is a magnificent performance, skillful and daring beyond measure; so instead of driving them off I asked for a seat in their long dugout to see how it was done. As we swept up and down the dangerous river, with pitch-pine blazing and cracking and the black shadows jumping about us, two woodcock sprang up from the shore and whirled madly around the pirogue. One brushed my face with his wings, and was driven away only when Sandy in the bow gave a mighty lunge of his spear and with a howl of exultation flung a twenty-pound, kicking salmon back into my lap. But several times that night I saw the flash of their wings, or heard their low surprised twitter above the crackle of the fire and the rush and roar of the rapids.

When he finds good feeding grounds on his southern migrations Whitooweek will stay with us, if undisturbed, until a sharp frost seals up his storehouse by making the ground too hard for his

sensitive bill to penetrate. Then he slips away southward to the next open spring or alder run. Not far away, on Shippan Point, is a little spring that rarely freezes and whose waters overflow and make a green spot even in midwinter. The point is well covered with houses now, but formerly it was good woodcock ground, and the little spring always welcomed a few of the birds with the welcome that only a spring can give. Last year, at Christmas time, I found a woodcock there quite at home, within a stone's throw of two or three houses and with snow lying deep all around him. He had lingered there weeks after all other birds had gone, either held by old associations and memories of a time when only the woodcock knew the place; or else, wounded and unable to fly, he had sought out the one spot in all the region where he might live and be fed until his wing should heal. Nature, whom men call cruel, had cared for him tenderly, healing his wounds that man had given, and giving him food and a safe refuge at a time when all other feeding-grounds were held

*Whitooweek
The Hermit*

fast in the grip of winter; but men, who can be kind and reasonable, saw no deep meaning in it all. The day after I found him a hunter passed that way, and was proud of having killed the very last woodcock of the season.

A WOODCOCK GENIUS

A Woodcock Genius

THERE is one astonishing thing about Whitooweek which can scarcely be called a habit, but which is probably the discovery of one or two rare individuals here and there more original than their fellows. Like the eider-ducks and the bear and the beaver, Whitooweek sometimes uses a rude kind of surgery for binding up his

A Woodcock Genius

wounds. Twenty years ago, while sitting quietly by a brook at the edge of the woods in Bridgewater, a woodcock suddenly fluttered out into the open and made his way to a spot on the bank where a light streak of sticky mud and clay showed clearly from where I was watching. It was the early hunting season and gunners were abroad in the land, and my first impression was that this was a wounded bird that had made a long flight after being shot, and that had now come out to the stream to drink or to bathe his wound. Whether this were so or not is a matter of guesswork; but the bird was acting strangely in broad daylight, and I crept nearer till I could see him plainly on the other side of the little stream, though he was still

too far away for me to be absolutely sure of
what all his motions meant.

At first he took soft clay in his bill from the
edge of the water and seemed to be smear-
ing it on one leg near the knee. Then he
fluttered away on one foot for a short distance and seemed to be pulling tiny roots
and fibers of grass, which he worked into
the clay that he had already smeared on his
leg. Again he took more clay and plas-
tered it over the fibers, putting on more and
more till I could plainly see the enlargement,
working away with strange, silent intentness
for fully fifteen minutes, while I watched and
wondered, scarce believing my eyes. Then
he stood perfectly still for a full hour under
an overhanging sod, where the eye could
with difficulty find him, his only motion
meanwhile being an occasional rubbing and
smoothing of the clay bandage with his bill,
until it hardened enough to suit him, whereupon he fluttered away from the brook and
disappeared in the thick woods.

I had my own explanation of the incredible action, namely, that the woodcock had a

broken leg, and had deliberately put it into a clay cast to hold the broken bones in place until they should knit together again; but naturally I kept my own counsel, knowing that no one would believe in the theory. For years I questioned gunners closely, and found two who said that they had killed woodcock whose legs had at one time been broken and had healed again. As far as they could remember, the leg had in each case healed perfectly straight instead of twisting out to one side, as a chicken's leg does when broken and allowed to knit of itself. I examined hundreds of woodcock in the markets in different localities, and found one whose leg had at one time been broken by a shot and then had healed perfectly. There were plain signs of dried mud at the break; but that was also true of the other leg near the foot, which only indicated that the bird had been feeding in soft places. All this proved nothing to an outsider, and I kept silence as to what I had seen until last winter, twenty years afterwards, when the confirmation came unexpectedly. I had been speaking of animals before the Contemporary Club of Bridgeport when a gentleman, a lawyer well known all over the state, came to me and told me eagerly of a curious find he had made the previous autumn. He was gunning one day with a friend, when they shot a woodcock, which on being brought in by the dog was found to have a lump of hard clay on one of its legs. Curious to know what it meant he chipped the clay off with his penknife and found a broken bone, which was then almost healed and as straight as ever. A few weeks later the bird, had he lived, would undoubtedly have taken off the cast himself and there would have been nothing to indicate anything unusual about him.

A Woodcock Genius

So I give the observation now, at last, since proof is at hand, not to indicate a new or old habit of Whitooweek, — for how far the strange knowledge is spread among the woodcock and the wading birds no man can say, — but simply to indicate how little we know of the inner life of the hermit, and indeed of all wild birds, and how much there is yet to be discovered when we shall lay aside the gun for the field-glass and learn to interpret the wonderful life which goes on unseen all about us.

WHEN
UPWEEKIS
GOES HUNTING

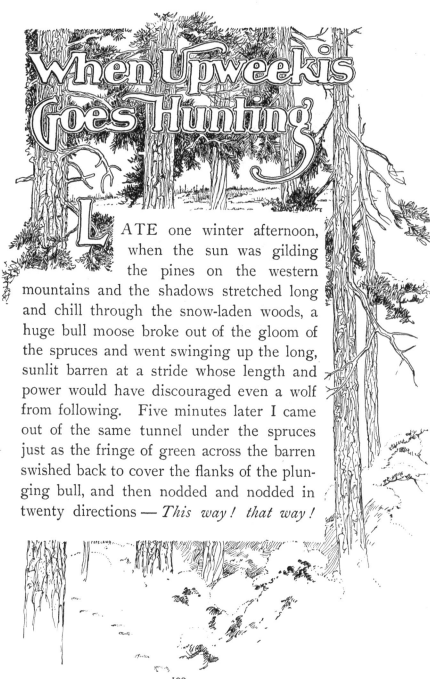

When Upweekis Goes Hunting

LATE one winter afternoon, when the sun was gilding the pines on the western mountains and the shadows stretched long and chill through the snow-laden woods, a huge bull moose broke out of the gloom of the spruces and went swinging up the long, sunlit barren at a stride whose length and power would have discouraged even a wolf from following. Five minutes later I came out of the same tunnel under the spruces just as the fringe of green across the barren swished back to cover the flanks of the plunging bull, and then nodded and nodded in twenty directions — *This way! that way!*

here! yonder! — to mislead any that might follow on his track. For at times even the hemlocks and the alders and the waters and the leaves and the creaking boughs and the dancing shadows all seem to conspire to shield the innocent Wood Folk from the hostile eyes and hands of those that pursue them. And that is one reason why it is so hard to see game in the woods.

The big moose had fooled me that time. When he knew that I was following him he ran far ahead, and then circled swiftly back to stand motionless in a hillside thicket within twenty yards of the trail that he had made scarcely an hour agone. There he could see perfectly, without being seen, what it was that was following him. When I came by, following swiftly and silently the deep tracks in the snow, he let me pass below him while he took a good look and a sniff at me; then he glided away like a shadow in the opposite direction.

Unfortunately a dead branch under the snow broke with a dull snap beneath his cautious hoof, and I turned aside to see — and so saved myself the long tramp up and down the cunning trails. When he saw that his trick was discovered he broke away for the open barren, with all his wonderful powers of eye and ear and tireless legs alert to save himself from the man whom he mistook for his deadly enemy.

It was of small use to follow him further, so I sat down on a prostrate yellow birch to rest and listen awhile in the vast silence, and to watch anything that might be passing through the cold white woods.

Under the fringe of evergreen the soft purple shadows jumped suddenly, and a hare as white as the snow bounded out. In long nervous jumps, like a bundle of wire springs, he went leaping before my face across a narrow arm of the barren to the shelter of a point below. The soft arms of the ground spruces and the softer shadows beneath them seemed to open of their own accord to let him in. All nodding of branches and dropping of snow pads and jumping of shadows ceased instantly, and all along the fringe of evergreen silent voices were saying, There is nothing here; we have not seen him; there is nothing here.

Now why did he run that way, I thought; for Moktaques is a crazy, erratic fellow, and never does things in a businesslike way unless he has to. As I wondered, there was a gleam of yellow fire under the purple shadows whence Moktaques had come, and the fierce round head of a Canada lynx was thrust out of the tunnel that the hare had made only a moment before. His big gray body had scarcely pushed itself into sight when the shadows stirred farther down the fringe of evergreen; another and another lynx glided out; and I caught my breath as five of the savage creatures swept across the narrow arm of the barren, each with his head thrust out, his fierce eyes piercing the gloom ahead like golden lances, and holding his place in the stately, appalling line of fierceness and power as silent as the shadow of death. My nerves tingled at the thought of what would happen to Moktaques when one of the line should discover and jump him.

Indeed, having no rifle, I was glad enough myself to sit very still and let the savage creatures go by without finding me.

The middle lynx, a fierce old female, was following the hare's trail; and in a moment it flashed across me who she was and what they were all doing. Here, at last, was the secret of the lynx bands that one sometimes finds in the winter woods, and that occasion-ally threaten or appall one with a ferocity that the individual animals never manifest. For Upweekis, though big and fierce, is at heart a slinking, cowardly, treacherous crea-ture — like all cats — and so loves best to be alone. Knowing that the rest of his tribe are like himself, he suspects them all and is fearful that in any division of common spoils somebody else would get the lion's share. And so I have never found among the cats any trace of the well-defined regulations that seem to prevail among nearly all other animals.

In winter, however, it is different. Then necessity compels Upweekis to lay aside some of his feline selfishness and hunt in savage bands. Every seven years, especially, when rabbits are scarce in the woods because of the sickness that kills them off periodically, you may stumble upon one of these pirate crews haunting the deer yards or following after the caribou herds; but until the ferocious line swept out of the purple shadows under my very eyes I had no idea that these bands are—almost invariably, as I have since learned —family parties that hold together through the winter, just as fawns follow the old doe until the spring comes, in order that her wisdom may find them food, and her superior strength break a way for them when snows are deep and enemies are hard at heel.

The big lynx in the middle was the mother; the four other lynxes were her cubs; and they held together now, partly that their imperfect education might be finished under her own eyes, but chiefly that in the hungry winter days they might combine their powers and hunt more systematically, and pull down, if need be, the larger animals that might defy them individually.

As she crossed the fresh trail of the bull moose the old mother lynx thrust her big head into it for a long sniff. The line closed up instantly and each lynx stood like a statue, his blunt nose down into a reeking hoof mark, studying through dull senses what it was that had just passed. The old lynx swung her head up and down the line of her motionless cubs; then with a ferocious snarl curling under her whiskers she pushed forward again. A score of starving lynxes all together would scarcely follow a bull of that stride and power. Only the smell of blood would drag them unwillingly along such a trail; and even then, if they overtook the author of it, they would only squat around him in a fierce solemn circle, yawning hungrily and hoping he would die. Now, somewhere just ahead, easier game was hiding. An unvoiced command seemed to run up and down the line of waiting cubs. Each thrust his head out at the same instant and the silent march went on.

When the last of the line had glided out of sight among the bushes of the point below,

When Upweekis Goes Hunting

**When Upweekis
Goes Hunting**

I ran swiftly through the woods, making no noise in the soft snow, and crouched motionless under the spruces on the lower side of the point, hoping to see the cunning hunters again. There was but a moment to wait. From under a bending evergreen tip Moktaques leaped out and went flying across the open for the next wooded point. Close behind him sounded a snarl, and with a terrific rush as she sighted the game the old lynx burst out, calling savagely to her line of hunters to close in. Like the blast of a squall they came, stretching out in enormous bounds and closing in from either end so as to cut off the circling run of the flying game. In a flash the two ends of the line had met and whirled in sharply; in another flash Moktaques was crouching close in the snow in the center of a fierce circle that rolled in upon him like a whirlwind. As the smallest lynx leaped for his game an electric shock seemed to touch the motionless hare. He shot forward as if galvanized, leaping high over the crouching terror before him, striving to break out of the terrible circle. Then the lynx over whose head he passed leaped straight up, caught the flying creature fairly in his great paws, fell over backwards, and was covered in an instant by the other lynxes that hurled themselves upon him like furies, snapping and clawing ferociously at the mouthful which he had pulled down at the very moment of its escape.

There was an appalling scrimmage for a moment; then, before I could fairly rub my eyes, the hare had vanished utterly, and a savage ring of lynxes were licking their chops hungrily, glaring and growling at each other to see which it was that had gotten the biggest mouthful.

When they disappeared at last, slinking away in a long line under the edge of the barren, I took up the back track to see how they had been hunting. For a full mile, straight back toward my camp, I followed the tracks and read the record of as keen a bit of bush beating as was ever seen in the woods. They had swept along all that distance in an almost perfect line, starting every living thing that lay athwart their path. Here it was a ruffed grouse that one had jumped for and missed, as the startled bird whirred away into the gloom. There one had climbed a tree and shaken something off into the snow, where the others licked up every morsel so clean that I could not tell what the unfortunate creature was; but a curious bit of savage daring was manifest, for the lynx that had gone up the tree after the game had hurled himself down like a catapult, leaving a huge hole in the snow, so as to be in at the death before his savage fellows, which had come flying in with great bounds, should have eaten everything and left not even a smell for his own share. And there, at last, at the very end of the line, another hare had been started and, running in a short circle, as hares often do, had been met and seized by the fourth lynx as the long line swung in swiftly to head him off.

Years later, and miles away on the Renous barrens, I saw another and more wonderful bit of the same keen hunting. From

a ridge above a small barren I saw a herd
of caribou acting strangely and went down
to investigate. As I reached the fringe of
thick bushes that lined the open I saw the
caribou cluster excitedly about the base of
a big rock across the barren, not more than
two hundred yards away. Something was
there, evidently, which excited their curiosity, — and caribou are the most inquisitive
creatures, at times, in all the woods, — but
I had to study the rock sharply through my
field-glasses before I made out the round
fierce head of a big lynx pressed flat against
the gray stone. One side of the rock was
almost perpendicular, rising sheer some fifteen or twenty feet above the plain; the
other side slanted off less abruptly toward
the woods; and the big lynx, which had
probably scrambled up from the woods to spy
on the caribou, was now hanging half over
the edge of rock, swaying his savage head
from side to side and stretching one wide
paw after another at the animals beneath.

The caribou were getting more excited
and curious every moment. Caribou are like

turkeys; when they see some new thing they must die or find out about it. Now they were spreading and closing their ranks, wavering back and forth, stretching ears and noses at the queer thing on the rock, but drawing nearer and nearer with every change.

Suddenly the lynx jumped, not at the caribou, for they were still too far away, but high in the air with paws outspread. He came down in a flurry of snow, whirled round and round as if bewitched, then vanished silently in two great jumps into the shelter of the nearest evergreens.

The caribou broke wildly at the strange sight, but turned after a startled bound or two to see what it was that had frightened them. There was nothing in sight, and like a flock of foolish sheep they came timidly back, nosing the snow and stretching their ears at the rock again; for there at the top was the big lynx, swinging his round head from side to side as before, and reaching his paws alternately at the herd, as if to show them how broad and fine they were.

Slowly the little herd neared the rock and the lynx drew back, as if to lure them on. They were full of burning curiosity, but they had seen one spring, at least, and measured its power, and so kept at a respectful distance. Then one young caribou left the others and went nosing along the edge of the woods to find the trail of the queer thing, or get to leeward of the rock, and so find out by smell — which is the only sure sense that a caribou possesses — what it was all about. A wind seemed to stir a dried tuft of grass on the summit of the great rock. I put my glasses upon it instantly, then caught my breath in suppressed excitement as I made out the tufted ears of two or three other lynxes crouching flat on their high tower, out of sight of the foolish herd, but watching every movement with fierce, yellow, unblinking eyes.

When Upweekis Goes Hunting

The young caribou found the trail, put his nose down into it, then started cautiously back toward the rock to nose the other hole in the snow and be sure that it smelled just like the first one. Up on the rock the big lynx drew further back; the herd pressed close, raising their heads high to see what he was doing; and the young caribou stole up and put his nose down into the trail again. Then three living catapults shot over the high rim of the rock and fell upon him. Like a flash the big lynx was on his feet, drawing himself up to his full height and hurling a savage screech of exultation after the flying herd. Then he, too, shot over the rock, fell fair on the neck of the struggling young caribou, and bore him down into the snow.

Upweekis is a stupid fellow. He will poke his big head into a wire noose as foolishly as any rabbit, and then he will fight savagely with the pole at the other end of the noose until he chokes himself. But no one could follow that wonderful trail in the snow, or sit with tingling nerves under the spruces watching that wild bit of fox-play, without a growing respect for the shadowy

" Then he, too, shot over
the rock "

creature of the big round tracks that wander, wander everywhere through the winter woods, and without wondering intensely in what kind of savage school Mother Upweekis trains her little ones.

K'DUNK THE FAT ONE

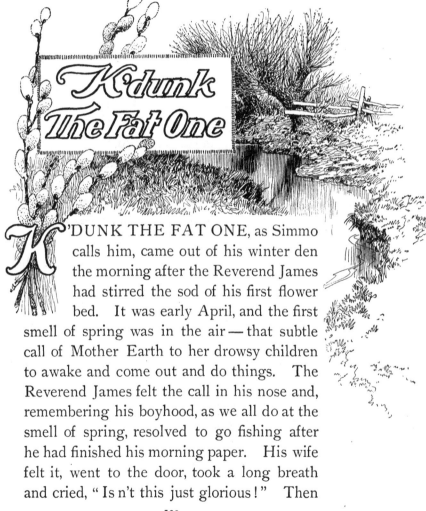

’DUNK THE FAT ONE, as Simmo calls him, came out of his winter den the morning after the Reverend James had stirred the sod of his first flower bed. It was early April, and the first smell of spring was in the air — that subtle call of Mother Earth to her drowsy children to awake and come out and do things. The Reverend James felt the call in his nose and, remembering his boyhood, as we all do at the smell of spring, resolved to go fishing after he had finished his morning paper. His wife felt it, went to the door, took a long breath and cried, "Is n't this just glorious!" Then

K'dunk
The Fat One

she grabbed a trowel — for when a man must off to the brook for his first trout a woman, by the same inner compulsion, must dig in the earth — and started for the flower bed. A moment later her excited call came floating in through the open window.

"Ja-a-a-a-mes? James!" — the first call with a long up slide, the second more peremptory — "what in the world did you plant in this flower bed?"

"Why," said the Reverend James, peering quizzically over the rim of his spectacles at the open window, "why, I thought I planted portulaca seed."

"Then come out here and see what's come up," ordered his wife; and the surprised old gentleman came hurriedly to the door to blink in astonishment at three fat toads that were also blinking in the warm sunshine, and a huge mud-turtle that was sprawling and hissing indignantly in a great hole in the middle of his flower bed.

A sly, whimsical twinkle was under the old minister's spectacles as he regarded the queer crop that had come up overnight.

"Whatsoever a man soweth, whatsoever a man soweth," he quoted softly to himself, eying the three toads askance, and poking the big turtle inquisitively, but snapping his hand back at sight and sound of the hooked beak and the fierce hissing. Then, because his library contained no book of exegesis equal to the occasion, he caught a small boy who was passing on his way to school and sent him off post-haste to my rooms to find out what it was all about.

Now the three fat toads had also smelled the spring down in a soft spot under the lawn, whither, in the previous autumn, they had burrowed for their winter sleep. When the Reverend James stirred the sod, the warm sun thawed them out and brought them the spring's message, and they scrambled up to the surface promptly, as full of new life as if they had not been frozen into insensible clods for the past six months. As for the big turtle, the smell of the fresh earth had probably brought her up from the neighboring pond to search out a nest for herself where she might lay her eggs. Finding the

K'dunk
The Fat
One

*Kdunk
The Fat
One*

soft warm earth of the portulaca bed, she
had squirmed and twisted her way down
into it, the loose earth tumbling in on her
and hiding her as she went down.

When the sharp feminine eyes swept over
the flower bed they detected at once the
hollow in the middle, showing careless work-
manship on the part of somebody. " That
hole must be filled up," promptly declared
Mrs. James; but first, woman-like, she thrust
her trowel deep into it. "Aha! a rock —
careless man," she gave judgment, and took
another jab and a two-handed
heave at the hard
object. Whereupon
out came the big mud-turtle, scrambling,
hissing, protesting with beak and claw
against being driven out of the best nest
she had ever found so early in the season.
That night there were curious sounds
in the grass and dead leaves —
rustlings and croakings and low
husky trills, as the toads came
hopping briskly by

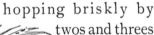

twos and threes

down to the pond. From every direction, from garden and lawn and wood and old stone wall, they came croaking and trilling through the quiet twilight, and hopping high with delight at the first smell of water. Down the banks they came, sliding, rolling, tumbling end over end, — any way to get down quickly, — landing at last with glad splashings and croakings in the warm shallows, where they promptly took to biting and clawing and absurd little wrestling bouts; which is the toad's way of settling his disputes and taking his own mate away from the other fellows.

Two or three days they stayed in the pond, filling the air with gurgling croaks and filling the water with endless strings of gelatine-coated eggs — enough to fill the whole pond banks-full of pollywogs, did not Mother Nature step in and mercifully dispose of ninety-nine per cent of them within a few days of hatching, and set the rest of them to eating each other industriously as they grew, till every pollywog that was left might truthfully sing with the cannibalistic mariner:

K'dunk the Fat One

K'dunk
The Fat One

Oh, I am the cook and the captain bold
And the mate of the Nancy brig,
The bo'sn tight and the midshipmite
And the crew of the captain's gig.

For every pollywog represented in his proper person some hundred or more of his fellow-pollywogs that he had eaten in the course of his development. But long before that time the toads had left the pond, scattering to the four winds whence they had come, caring not now what became of their offspring. It was then that K'dunk the Fat One came back to the portulaca bed.

Mrs. James found him there the next morning — a big, warty gray toad with a broad grin and a fat belly and an eye like a jewel — blinking sleepily after his night's hunting. "Mercy! there's that awful toad again. I hope" — with a cautious glance all round — "I hope he hasn't brought the turtle with him." She gave him a prod and a flip with the trowel to get him out of the flower bed, whereupon K'dunk scrambled into his hole under an overhanging sod and refused to come out, spite of tentative pokes

of the trowel in a hand that was altogether
too tender to hurt him.   And there he
stayed, waging his silent warfare against the
trowel, until I chanced along and persuaded
the good lady that she was trying to drive
away the very best friend that her flowers
could possibly have.   Then K'dunk settled
down in peace, and we all took to watching him.

His first care was to make a few hiding
holes here and there in the garden.   Most
of these were mere hollows in the soft
earth, where K'dunk would crouch with eyes
shut tight whenever his enemies were near.
His color changed rapidly till it was the
same general hue as his surroundings, so
that, when he lay quiet and shut his bright
eyes in one of his numerous hollows, it was
almost impossible to find him.   But after he
had been worried two or three times by the
house-dog — a fat, wheezy little pug that
always grew excited when K'dunk began to
hop about in the twilight but that could
never bark himself up to the point of touching the clammy thing with his nose — he

dug other holes, under the sod banks, or beside a rock, where Grunt, the pug, could not bother him without getting too much out of breath.

We made friends with him at first by scratching his back with a stick, at which pleasant operation he would swell and grunt with satisfaction. But you could never tell when he would get enough, or at what moment he would feel his dignity touched in a tender spot and go hopping off to the garden in high dudgeon. Then we fed him flies and bits of tender meat, which we would wiggle with a bit of grass to make them seem alive. At the same time we whistled a certain call to teach him when his supper was ready. Then, finally, by gentle handlings and pettings he grew quite tame, and at the sound of the whistle would scramble out from under the door-step, where he lived by day, and hop briskly in our direction to be fed and played with.

Though K'dunk had many interesting traits, which we discovered with amazement as the summer progressed and we grew better acquainted, I think that his feeding ways and tricks were the source of our most constant delight and wonder. Just to see him stalk a fly filled one with something of the tense excitement of a deer hunt. As he sat by a stump or clod in the fading light, some belated fly or early night-bug would light on the ground in front of him. Instantly the jewel eye in K'dunk's head would begin to flash and sparkle. He would crouch down and creep nearer, toeing in like a duck, slower and slower, one funny little paw brushing cautiously by the other, with all the stealth and caution of a cat stalking a chipmunk on the wall. Then, as he neared his game, there would be a bright flash of the jewel; a red streak shot through the air, so quick that your eye could not follow it, and the fly would disappear. Whereupon K'dunk would gulp something down, closing his eyes solemnly as he did so, as if he were saying grace, or as if, somehow, closing his eyes to all outward things made the morsel taste better.

K'dunk the Fat One

K'dunk *The Fat One*

The red streak, of course, was K'dunk's tongue, wherein lies the secret of his hunting. It is attached at the outer rim of his mouth, and folds back in his throat. The inner end is broad and soft and sticky, and he snaps it out and back quick as a wink or a lizard. Whatever luckless insect the tongue touches is done with all bothering of our humanity. The sticky tongue snaps him up and back into K'dunk's wide mouth before he has time to spread a wing or even to think what is the matter with him.

Once I saw him stalk a grasshopper, a big lively green fellow that, in a particularly long jump, had come out of the protecting grass and landed on the brown earth directly in front of where K'dunk was catching the flies that were coming in a steady stream to a bait that I had put out for them. Instantly K'dunk turned his attention from the flies to the larger game. Just as his tongue shot out the grasshopper, growing suspicious, jumped for cover. The soft tongue missed him by a hair, but struck one of his trailing legs and knocked him aside. In an instant

"The soft tongue struck one of his
trailing legs"

K'dunk was after him again, his legs scrambling desperately, his eyes blazing, and his tongue shooting in and out like a streak of flame. Just as the grasshopper rose in a hard jump the tongue hit him, and I saw no more. But K'dunk's gulp was bigger and his eyes were closed for a longer period than usual, and there was a loud protesting rustle in his throat as the grasshopper's long legs went kicking down the road that has no turning.

A big caterpillar that I found and brought to K'dunk one day afforded us all another field for rare observation. The caterpillar was a hairy fellow, bristling with stiff spines, and I doubted that the tongue had enough mucilage on it to stick to him. But K'dunk had no such doubts. His tongue flew out and his eyes closed solemnly. At the same time I saw the caterpillar shrink himself together and stick his spines out stiffer than ever. Then a curious thing came out, namely, that K'dunk's mouth is so big and his game is usually so small that he cannot taste his morsel; he just swallows mechanically, as if

Kdunk
The Fat
One

he were so used to catching his game that it never occurred to him that he could miss. When he opened his eyes and saw the caterpillar in the same place, he thought, evidently, that it was another one which had come in mysteriously on wings, as the flies were coming to my bait. Again his tongue shot out, and his eyes closed in a swallow of delight. But there in front of him, as his eyes opened, was another caterpillar. Such perfect harmony of supply and demand was never known to a toad before.

Again and again his tongue shot out, and each shot was followed by a blink and a gulp. All the while that he kept up this rapid shooting he thought he was getting fresh caterpillars; and all the while the hairy fellow was shrinking closer and closer together and sticking his spines out like a porcupine. But he was getting more mucilage on him at every shot. "That caterpillar is getting too stuck-up to live," presently said little Johnnie, who was watching the game with me; and at the word a hairy ball shot into the wide mouth that was yawning for him, and K'dunk went back to his fly-catching.

It is probably this lack of taste on K'dunk's part that accounts for the astonishing variety in his food. Nothing in the shape of an insect seemed to come amiss to him. Flies, wasps, crickets, caterpillars, doodle-bugs, and beetles of every description were all treated alike to the same red flash of his tongue and the blinking gulp. A half-dozen boys and girls, who were watching the queer pet with me, were put to their wits' end to find something that he would not eat. One boy, who picked huckleberries, brought in three or four of the disagreeable little bugs, known without a name by every country boy, that have the skunk habit of emitting overpowering odors when disturbed, thinking that he had found a poser for our pet; but K'dunk gobbled them up as if they had been set before him as a relish to tickle his appetite. Another brought potato bugs; but these too were fish for K'dunk's net. Then a third boy, who had charge of a kitchen garden,

K'dunk
The Fat One

went away wagging his head and saying that he had just picked something that no living thing would eat. When he came back he had a horse-radish bottle that swarmed with squash-bugs, twenty or thirty of the vile-smelling things, which he dumped out on the ground and stirred up with a stick.

Somebody ran and brought K'dunk from one of his hiding-places and set him down on the ground in front of the squirming mess. For a moment he seemed to be eying his proposition with astonishment. Then he crouched down and the swift red tongue-play began. In four minutes, by my watch, every squash-bug that stirred had disappeared, and K'dunk finished the others as fast as we could wiggle them with a straw to make them seem alive.

We gave up trying to beat him on variety after that, and settled down to the apparently simple task of trying to find out how many insects he could eat before calling halt. But even here K'dunk was too much for us; we never, singly or all together, reached the limit of his appetite. Once we fed him ninety rose-bugs without stopping. Another afternoon, when three boys appeared at the same hour, we put our catch together, a varied assortment of flies, bugs, and creeping things, a hundred and sixty-four head all told. Before dark K'dunk had eaten them all, and went hopping off to the garden on his night's hunting—as if he had not already done enough to prove himself our friend for the entire summer.

K'dunk The Fat One

Later we adopted a different plan and made the game come to K'dunk on its own wings, instead of running all over creation ourselves to catch it for him. Near the barn was a neglected drain where the flies were numerous enough to warn us to look after our sanitation more zealously. Here I built a little cage of wire netting, in which I placed a dead rat and some scraps from the table. When the midday sun found them and made them odorous, big flies began to pour in, with the loud buzzing which seems to be a signal to their fellows; for in ordinary flight the same flies are almost noiseless. Once,

however, they find a bit of carrion fit for their eggs, they buzz about loudly every few minutes, and other flies hear them; whereupon their quiet flight changes to a loud buzzing. So the news spreads — at least this seems to help the matter — and flies pour in from every direction.

At three o'clock I brought K'dunk from his meditations under the door-step and set him down in the cage, screening him with a big rhubarb leaf so that the sun would not dazzle his eyes too much. Then I took out my watch and sat down on a rock to count.

In the first ten minutes K'dunk got barely a dozen flies. They were wary of him in the bright light, and he was not yet waked up to the occasion. Then he crouched down between the rat and the scraps, worked a hollow for himself where he could turn without being noticed, and the red tongue-play began in earnest. In the next half hour he got sixty-six flies, an average of over two a minute. In an hour his record was a hundred and ten; and before I left him he had added two dozen more to the score of our enemies.

Then the flies ceased coming, as the air grew cool, and I carried him back to the door-step. But that night, later than usual, he was off to the garden again to keep up his splendid work.

K'dunk the Fat One

When the summer glow-worms came (lightning-bugs the boys called them) we saw another curious and pretty bit of hunting. One night, as we sat on the porch in the soft twilight, I saw the first lightning-bug glowing in the grass, and went to catch it as a jewel for a lady's hair. As I reached down my hand under a bush, the glow suddenly disappeared, and I put my fingers on K'dunk instead. He, too, had seen the glow and had instantly adopted jacking as his mode of hunting.

Later I caught a lightning-bug and put it in a tiny bottle, and dropped it in front of K'dunk as he started across the lawn in the late twilight. He saw the glow through the glass and took a shot at it promptly. As with the hairy caterpillar, he shut his eyes as he gulped down the imaginative morsel, and when he

**K'dunk
The Fat One**

opened them again there was another light-ning-bug glowing in the grass just where the first had been. So he kept the tiny bot-tle jumping about the lawn at the repeated laps of his tongue, blinking and swallowing betweenwhiles until the glow-worm, made dizzy perhaps by the topsy-turvy play of his strange cage, folded his wings and hid his little light. Whereupon K'dunk hopped away, thinking, no doubt, in his own way, that while lightning-bugs were unusually thick that night and furnished the prettiest kind of hunting, they were very poor satis-faction to a hungry stomach, — not to be compared with what he could get by jumping up at the insects that hid on the under side of the leaves on every plant in the garden.

It needed no words of mine by this time to convince the good Mrs. James that K'dunk was her friend. Indeed she paid a small boy ten cents apiece for a half dozen toads to turn loose about the premises to help K'dunk in his excellent work.

And the garden flourished as never before, thanks to the humble little helpers. But K'dunk's virtues were more than utilitarian; he was full of unexpected things that kept us all constantly watching with delight to see what would happen next. As I said, he soon learned to come to the call; but more than that, he was fond of music. If you whistled a little tune softly, he would stay perfectly still until you finished before going off on his night's hunting. Then, if you changed the tune, or whistled discordantly, he would hop away as if he had no further use for you.

Sometimes, at night, a few young people would gather on the porch and sing together, — a proceeding which often tolled K'dunk out from under the door-step, and which, on one occasion, brought him hopping hurriedly back from the garden, whither he had gone an hour before to hunt his supper. Quiet hymns he seemed to like, for he always kept still as a worshiper, — which pleased the Reverend James immensely, — but " rag-time " music he detested, if one could judge by his

K'dunk
The Fat
One

actions and by the unmistakable way he had
of turning his back upon what did not appeal
to him or touch his queer fancy.

One evening a young girl with a very
sweet natural voice was singing by an open
window on the porch. She was singing for
the old folks' pleasure, that night, some old
simple melodies that they liked best. Just
within the window the piano was playing a
soft accompaniment. A stir in the grass attracted my attention, and there was K'dunk
trying in vain to climb up the step. I called
Mrs. James' attention quietly to the queer
guest, and then lifted K'dunk gently to the
piazza. There he followed along the rail until
he was close beside the singer, where he sat
perfectly still, listening intently as long as she
sang. Nor was she conscious that night of
this least one among her hearers.

Two or three times this happened in the
course of the summer. The girl's voice
seemed to have a fascination for our homely
little pet, for at the first sweet notes he
would scramble out from his hiding and
try to climb the steps. When I lifted him

to the porch he would hop along till close beside the singer, where he would sit, all quietness and appreciation, as long as she sang. Then, one night when he had sat humble and attentive at her feet through two songs, a tenor who studied in New York, and who sometimes gave concerts, was invited to sing. He responded promptly and atrociously with "O Hully Gee," — which was not the name of the thing, but only the academy boys' version of a once popular love-song. Had K'dunk been a German choir-leader he could not have so promptly and perfectly expressed his opinion of the wretched twaddle. It was not the fool words, which he could not fortunately understand, nor yet the wretched tingle-tangle music, which was past praying for, but rather the voice itself with its forced unnatural quality so often affected by tenors. At the first strident notes K'dunk grew uneasy. Then he scrambled to the edge of the porch and fell off headlong in his haste to get down and away from the soul-disturbing performance.

K'dunk the Fat One

K'dunk
The Fat One

The sudden flight almost caused a panic and an awful breach of hospitality among the few who were quietly watching things. To cover an irrepressible chuckle I slipped away after K'dunk, who scrambled clear to the pie-plant patch before he stopped hopping. As I went I heard the gentle Mrs. James, soul of goodness and hospitality, coughing violently into her handkerchief, as if a rude draught had struck her sensitive throat; but it sounded to me more like a squirrel that I once heard snickering inside of a hollow pumpkin. However, the tenor sang on, and all was well. K'dunk meanwhile was engaged in the better task of ridding the garden of noxious bugs, sitting up at times, in a funny way he had, and scratching the place where his ear should be.

It was soon after this, when we all loved K'dunk better than ever, that the most astonishing bit of his queer life came to the surface. Unlike the higher orders of animals, K'dunk receives no training whatever from his elders. The lower orders live so simple a life that instinct is enough for

them; and so Nature, who can be provident at times, as well as wasteful, omits the superfluous bother of teaching them. But many things he did before our eyes for which instinct could never account, and many difficulties arose for which innate knowledge was not sufficient; and then we saw his poor dull wits at work against the unexpected problems of the universe.

K'dunk The Fat One

As the summer grew hotter and hotter K'dunk left the door-step and made for himself a better den. All toads do this in the scorching days — hollow out a retreat under a sod or root or rotten stump, and drowse there in its cool damp shade while the sun blisters overhead. Just in front of the doorstep some broad flagstones extended across the lawn to the sidewalk. The frosts of many winters had forced them apart, some more and some less, and a ribbon of green grass now showed between many pairs of the stones. Where the ribbon was widest K'dunk found out, in some way, that the thin sod covered a hollow underneath, and he worked at this until the sod gave way

154

K'dunk
The Fat
One

and he tumbled into a roomy cavern under one of the flagstones. Here it was always cool, and he abandoned the door-step forthwith, sleeping through the drowsy August days in the better place that his wits had discovered.

Now K'dunk, with good hunting in the garden and with much artificial feeding at our hands, grew fatter and fatter. At times when he came hopping home in the morning, swelled out enormously with the uncounted insects that he had eaten, he found the space between the flagstones uncomfortably narrow. Other toads have the same difficulty and, to avoid it, simply scratch the entrance to their dens a little wider; but dig and push as he would, K'dunk could not budge the flagstones.

He scratched a longer entrance after his first hard squeezing, but that did no good; the doorway was still uncomfortably narrow, and he often reminded me, going into his house, of a very fat and pompous man trying to squeeze through a turnstile, tugging and pushing and tumbling through with a

grunt at last, and turning to eye the inven-
tion indignantly. To get out of his den
was easy, for during the long day he had
digested his dinner and was thin again; but
how to get in comfortably in the morning
with a full stomach, — that was the question.

Kdunk the Fat One

One morning I saw him come out of the
garden, and I knew instantly that he had
more trouble ahead. He had found some
rich nests of bugs that night and had eaten
enormously; his "fair round body" dragged
along the grass as he crawled rather than
hopped to his doorway, and his one desire
seemed to be to tumble into his den drowsily and go to sleep. But alas! he could not
get in. He had reached the limit at last.

First he put his head and shoulders
through, and by pulling at the under side
of the flagstones tried to hitch and coax
his way in. All in vain! His fat body
caught between the obstinate flags and only
wedged tighter and tighter. The bulging
part without was so much bigger than the
part within that he must have given it
up at a glance, could he only have seen

K'dunk
The Fat One

himself. But he worked away with wonderful patience till he knew it was of no use, when he pushed himself out again and sat looking into his inhospitable doorway, blinking and tousled and all covered with dust and grass roots. As he sat he kept scratching the place where his ear should be, as if he were thinking.

In a moment or two, as if he had solved the problem, he turned around and hitched his hind legs into the hole. He was going in backwards, but carefully, awkwardly, as if he were not used to it. This, however, was worse than the other, for his obstinate belly only wedged the tighter and, with a paw down on either side of him, every push lifted him up instead of pulling him down. He gave up quicker than before, because his head was out now and he could see better how he was progressing. At last he lay down, as if he had solved the problem, and tried to squirm through his long doorway lengthwise. This was better. He could get either his hind legs or his head and shoulders through;

but, like the buckets in the well, when one
end was down the other end was up, and still
his fat, obstinate body refused to go through
with the rest. Still he seemed to be making
progress, for every teeter of head and legs
worked his uncomfortable dinner into better
shape. At the end he wedged himself too
tight, and there was a harder scramble to get
out than there had been to get in. By a
desperate push and kick he freed himself
at last and sat, all tousled again, blinking
into his doorway, meditating.

Suddenly he turned and lowered his hind
legs into the hole. He was more careful
this time, afraid of being caught. When
he had dropped through as far as he could
go, he sat very still for some moments, supporting himself with a paw on either side.
His jaws opened slowly — and full of wonder at a curious twitching motion he was
making, I crept near on hands and knees
and looked down into his wide-open mouth.
There was his dinner, all sorts of flies and
night-bugs, coming up little by little and
being held in his great mouth as in a basket,

Kdunk the
Fat One

K'dunk The Fat One

while his stomach worked below and sent up supplies to relieve the pressure.

Slowly he slipped down as the stones began to lose their hard grip. A squirm, a twist, a comfortable roll of his stomach, a sudden jounce — and the thing was done. K'dunk was resting with a paw on either flagstone, his body safe below and his mouth, still wide open above, holding its precious contents, like an old-fashioned valise that had burst open. Then he swallowed his disturbed dinner down again in big gulps, and with a last scramble disappeared into his cool den.

That night he did not come out, but the second night he was busy in the garden as usual. To our deep regret he deserted both the door-step and the den with its narrow opening under the flagstones. It may be that in his own way he had pondered the problem of what might have become of him had the owl been after him when he came home that morning; for when I found him again he was safe under the hollow roots of an old apple-tree, where the entrance was wide enough to tumble in quickly, however much he had eaten. And there he stayed by day as long as I kept tabs on him.

K'dunk the Fat One

There was but one more interesting trait that I discovered in the last days of the summer, and that was his keenness in finding the best hunting-grounds. Just behind his den in the old apple-tree was a stone wall, under which insects of all kinds were plenty. K'dunk's den was on the east side, so that the sun as it set threw the cool shade of the wall over the place and brought our pet out earlier than was his wont. In some way he found out that the west side of the wall caught and held the sun's last rays, and that flies and all sorts of insects would light or crawl on the hot stones to get warm in the late afternoon. He made a tunnel for himself under the wall, just behind his den, and would lie close beside a certain gray stone on the west side, his gray color hiding him perfectly, picking off the flies as they lit with the quickness and certainty of a lizard. When bugs and insects crawled out of their

K'dunk
The Fat One

holes to sun themselves awhile on a warm stone, K'dunk, whose eye ranged up and down over his hunting-ground, would lie still until they settled comfortably, and would then creep cautiously within range and snap them up with a flash of his tongue that the eye could scarcely follow. In a dozen afternoons, watching him there, I never saw him miss a single shot, while the number of flies and insects he destroyed must have reached up into the hundreds.

In the same field four or five cows were pastured, and on pleasant days they were milked out of doors instead of being driven into the barn. Now those who have watched cows at milking time have probably noted how the flies swarm on their legs, clustering thickly above the hoofs, where the switching of a nervous tail cannot disturb them. K'dunk had noted it too, and often during the milking, when the cows were quiet, he would approach a certain animal out of the herd, creep up on one hoof after another and snap off every fly within reach. Then he would jump for the highest ones, hitting them almost invariably, and tumble off on his back after a successful shot. But in a moment he had scrambled back on a hoof again and was waiting for the next fly to light within range. The most curious part of it all was that he attached himself to one cow, and would seek her out of the herd wherever she was being milked. He never, so far as I observed, went near any of the others; and the cow after a time seemed to recognize the toad as a friend, and would often stand still after being milked as long as K'dunk remained perched on one of her hoofs.

As the summer waned and green things disappeared from the garden he deserted that also, going wider and wider afield in his night's hunting. He grew wilder, too, as all things do in the autumn days, till at last no whistle, however loud, would bring him back. Whether the owl caught him, or whether he still looks forward to the long life that Nature gives to the toads, I do not know; but under the edge of the portulaca bed, as I write, is a suspicious

K'dunk The Fat One

hollow that the frosts and snows have not quite concealed. I shall watch that in the spring with more than common interest to know whether K'dunk the Fat One remembers his old friends.

MOOWEEN'S DEN

Mooween's Den

ONE day, in a long tramp through the heavy forest that borders the Little Southwest River, I came upon a dim old road that had been bushed the previous winter and, having nothing better to do, followed it to see whither it would lead me. Other feet than mine had recently gone on the same errand, for every soft spot in the earth, every moldering log and patch of swamp moss and muddy place beside the brook, had deep footprints and claw marks to tell me that Mooween the bear had gone back and forth many times

Mooween's Den

over the same trail. Then I knew what I would find at the other end of it, and was not at all surprised when it led me to the open yard of a big lumber camp beside the river.

There is always a fascination in such places, where men have lived their simple lives in the heart of the woods, shut out from all the rest of the world during the long winter; so I began to prowl quietly about the shanties to see what I could find. The door of the low stable swung invitingly open, but it was a dark, musty, ill-smelling place now, though cozy enough in winter, and only the porcupines had invaded it. I left it after a glance and came round to the men's shanty.

The door of this was firmly locked; but a big hole had been torn in the roof by bears, and I crawled in by that entrance. Mooween had been here many times ahead of me. Every corner of the big room, the bunks and the cupboards and even the stove, had been ransacked from one end to the other; and the strong, doggy smell of a bear was everywhere, showing how recently

" Mooween had been here many times
ahead of me "

he had searched the place. Here in a corner a large tin box had been wrenched open,
and flour was scattered over the floor and
deacon-seat, as if a whirlwind had struck the
place. Mooween was playful evidently; or
perhaps he was mad that the stuff for which
he had taken so much trouble was too dry
to eat. The white print of one paw was
drawn everywhere on the floor and walls.
This was the paw of a little bear, who had
undoubtedly come late, and had to be content with what the others had left.

All over the log floor some cask or vessel
had been rolled about before the flour was
spilled, and I knew instantly that I was on
the track of the first bear that entered, the
big fellow that had torn the hole in the roof
and had then nosed all over the camp without disturbing anything until he found what
he wanted. As the thing was rolled about
under his paw the contents had been spilled
liberally, and Mooween had followed it about,
lapping up what he found on the floor and
leaving not a single drop to tell the story;
but from the flies that gathered in clusters

in every sunny spot I knew that the stuff must have been sweet — molasses probably — and that Mooween, after he had eaten it all, had carried away the pail or jug to lick it clean, as bears almost invariably do when they sack a lumber camp.

Other bears had followed him into the camp and found poor pickings. One had thumped open a half barrel of pork and sampled the salty contents, and then had nosed a pile of old moccasins inquisitively. A dozen axes and peaveys had been pulled out of a barrel and thrown on the floor, to see if perchance they had hidden anything good to eat. Every pot and pan in the big cupboard had been taken out and given a lap or two to find out what they had cooked last; and one bear had stood up on his hind legs and swept off the contents of a high shelf with a sweep of his paw. Altogether the camp had been sacked thoroughly, and it was of little use for any other bear to search the place. The camp seemed to be waiting silently for the lumbermen to come back in the fall and set things to rights.

I crawled back through the hole in the roof and began to search the big yard carefully. If Mooween had carried anything outside, it would be found not far away; and there is a keen interest, for me at least, in finding anything that the Wood Folk have touched or handled. The alder stick that the beaver cut yesterday, or the little mud pie that his paws have patted smooth; the knot that the young coons have used as a plaything in their den to beguile the hours when their mother was away; the tree against which two or three bears have measured and scratched their height; the log where the grouse drums; the discarded horn of a moose; the track of an unknown beast; the old den of a lucivee, — in all these things, and a thousand more, there is I know not what fascination that draws me a mile out of my course just to stand for a moment where wild little feet have surely passed and to read the silent records they have left behind them.

In front of the camp door was a huge pile of chips where the lumbermen had chopped their wood during the long winter. I walked up on this, wondering at its huge size and making a great clatter as the chips slipped from under me. Suddenly there was a terrifying rumble at my feet. A bear burst out of the chip pile, as if he had been blown up by an explosion, and plunged away headlong into the silent woods.

This was startling enough on a quiet day. I had been looking for something that Mooween had left, not for Mooween himself. I stood stock still where I was on the chip pile, staring after the bear, wondering first where he came from, and then wondering what would have happened had he been inside the shanty when I came in through the roof. Then I came down and found the queerest den that ever I have stumbled upon in the woods.

On the north side of the mound a tunnel a couple of feet long had been dug by the bear, and the heart of the chip pile had been thrown out to make a little cave, just big enough for Mooween to lie down in. I poked my head into it, and to my astonishment

found it to be a regular ice house, with
snow and ice packed in solidly among
the chips. I tried the pile in other places
and found the same conditions everywhere.
A foot or two beneath the surface the ice
remained as perfectly preserved as if it were
January instead of midsummer. Here were
shade and coolness such as no sun could
disturb, and in a moment it came to me how
the queer thing had come about.

All winter long the lumbermen had
chopped their fire-wood on the same spot,
using axes only, and making an enormous
amount of chips and rubbish. When heavy
snows fell, instead of clearing it away, they
simply cut more wood on top of it, tramp-
ing the snow beneath into a solid mass and
covering it over with fresh chips. So the pile
grew,—first a layer of chips, then a thick
blanket of snow, then more chips and snow
again,—growing bigger and bigger until in
April the lumbermen locked their shanty
and went out on the spring drive of logs.

When the spring sun melted the snow in
the woods the big pile remained, settling

slowly as the days warmed. At midday the top layer of snow would melt and trickle down through the chips; by night it would freeze hard, gradually changing the snow within to soft ice. When all the snow in the woods was gone, that in the chip pile remained, kept from melting by the thick wooden blankets that covered it; and the longest summer would hardly be sufficient to melt it down to the bottom layer, which represented the first fall of snow in the previous autumn.

When I found the spot it was early July. The sun was blistering hot overhead, and the flies and mosquitoes were out in myriads; but in Mooween's den two or three layers of ice were as yet unmelted. The hole was as cold as a refrigerator, and not a fly of any kind would stay there for a single second.

At the inner end of the den something glimmered as my eyes grew accustomed to the gloom, and I reached in my hand and pulled the thing out. It was a stone jug, and I knew instantly what had held the molasses that had been spilled on the camp

floor. Mooween had probably pulled the
cork and rolled the jug about, lapping up
the contents as they came out. When he
could get no more he had taken the jug
under his arm as he climbed through the
hole in the roof, and kept it now in his cool
den to lick it all over again for any stray
drops of molasses that he might have overlooked. Perhaps also he found comfort in
putting his tongue or his nose into the
nozzle-mouth to smell the sweetness that
he could no longer reach.

I have found one or two strange winter
dens of Mooween, and have followed his trail
uncounted miles through the snow when he
had been driven out of one *hibernaculum*
and was seeking another in the remote fast-
nesses, making an unending trail with the
evident intention of tiring out any hunter
who should attempt to follow him. I have
found his bathing pools repeatedly, and
watched him in midsummer when he
sought out cool retreats — a muddy eddy
in a trout brook under the alders, a mossy
hollow under the north side of a great sheer

ledge — to escape the flies and heat. But none of them compare with this lumberman's ice house which his wits had appropriated, and which, from many signs about the place, he was accustomed to use daily for his nap when the sun was hottest; and none of his many queer traits ever appealed to me quite so strongly as the humorous cunning which prompted him to take the jug with him into his den. It was safe there, whether Mooween were at home or not, for no bear will ever enter another's den unless the owner first show him in; and while other bears were in the hot camp, trying to find a satisfactory bite of salt pork and dry flour, Mooween was lying snug in his ice house licking the molasses jug that represented his own particular share of the plunder.

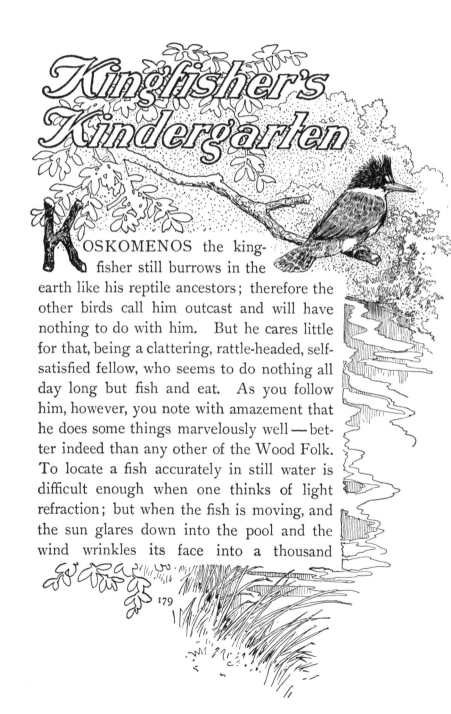

Kingfisher's Kindergarten

KOSKOMENOS the king-
fisher still burrows in the
earth like his reptile ancestors; therefore the
other birds call him outcast and will have
nothing to do with him. But he cares little
for that, being a clattering, rattle-headed, self-
satisfied fellow, who seems to do nothing all
day long but fish and eat. As you follow
him, however, you note with amazement that
he does some things marvelously well — better indeed than any other of the Wood Folk.
To locate a fish accurately in still water is
difficult enough when one thinks of light
refraction; but when the fish is moving, and
the sun glares down into the pool and the
wind wrinkles its face into a thousand

179

flashing, changing furrows and ridges,—then the bird that can point a bill straight to his fish and hit him fair just behind the gills must have more in his head than the usual chattering gossip that one hears from him on the trout streams.

This was the lesson that impressed itself upon me when I first began to study Koskomenos; and the object of this little sketch, which records those first strong impressions, is not to give our kingfisher's color or markings or breeding habits — you can get all that from the bird books — but to suggest a possible answer to the question of how he learns so much, and how he teaches his wisdom to the little kingfishers.

Just below my camp, one summer, was a trout pool. Below the trout pool was a shaded minnow basin, a kind of storehouse for the pool above, where the trout foraged in the early and late twilight, and where, if you hooked a red-fin delicately on a fine leader and dropped it in from the crotch of an overhanging tree, you might sometimes catch a big one.

"He drove off a mink and almost killed
the savage creature"

Early one morning, while I was sitting in the tree, a kingfisher swept up the river and disappeared under the opposite bank. He had a nest in there, so cunningly hidden under an overhanging root that till then I had not discovered it, though I had fished the pool and seen the kingfishers clattering about many times. They were unusually noisy when I was near, and flew up-stream over the trout pool with a long, rattling call again and again — a ruse, no doubt, to make me think that their nest was somewhere far above.

I watched the nest closely after that, in the intervals when I was not fishing, and learned many things to fill one with wonder and respect for this unknown, clattering outcast of the wilderness rivers. He has devotion for his mate, and feeds her most gallantly while she is brooding. He has courage, plenty of it. One day, under my very eyes, he drove off a mink and almost killed the savage creature. He has well-defined fishing regulations and enforces them rigorously, never going beyond his limits and permitting no poaching on his own minnow pools. He also has fishing lore enough in his frowsy head — if one could get it out — to make Izaak Walton's discourse like a child's babble. Whether the wind be south or northeast, whether the day be dull or bright, he knows exactly where the little fish will be found, and how to catch them.

When the young birds came, the most interesting bit of Koskomenos' life was manifest. One morning as I sat watching, hidden away in the bushes, the mother kingfisher put her head out of her hole and looked about very anxiously. A big water-snake lay stretched along a stranded log on the shore. She pounced upon him instantly and drove him out of sight. Just above, at the foot of the trout pool, a brood of sheldrake were croaking and splashing about in the shallows. They were harmless, yet the kingfisher rushed upon them, clattering and scolding like a fishwife, and harried them all away into a quiet bogan.

On the way back she passed over a frog, a big, sober, sleepy fellow, waiting on a lily-pad for his sun-bath. Chigwooltz might catch young trout, and even little birds as they came to drink, but he would surely never molest a brood of kingfishers; yet the mother, like an irate housekeeper flourishing her broom at every corner of an unswept room, sounded her rattle loudly and dropped on the sleepy frog's head, sending him sputtering and scrambling away into the mud, as if Hawahak the hawk were after him. Then with another look all round to see that the stream was clear, and with a warning rattle to any Wood Folk that she might have overlooked, she darted into her nest, wiggling her tail like a satisfied duck as she disappeared.

After a moment a wild-eyed young kingfisher put his head out of the hole for his first look at the big world. A push from behind cut short his contemplation, and without any fuss whatever he sailed down to a dead branch on the other side of the stream. Another and another followed in the same way, as if each one had been told just what to do and where to go, till the whole family were sitting a-row, with the rippling stream below them and the deep blue heavens and the rustling world of woods above.

That was their first lesson, and their reward was near. The male bird had been fishing since daylight; now he began to bring minnows from an eddy where he had stored them, and to feed the hungry family and assure them, in his own way, that this big world, so different from the hole in the bank, was a good place to live in, and furnished no end of good things to eat.

The next lesson was more interesting, the lesson of catching fish. The school was a quiet, shallow pool with a muddy bottom against which the fish showed clearly, and with a convenient stub leaning over it from which to swoop. The old birds had caught a score of minnows, killed them, and dropped them here and there under the stub. Then they brought the young birds, showed them their game, and told them by repeated examples to dive and get it. The little fellows were hungry and took to the sport keenly; but one was timid, and only after the mother had twice dived and brought up a fish —

which she showed to the timid one and then dropped back in a most tantalizing way — did he muster up resolution to take the plunge.

A few mornings later, as I prowled along the shore, I came upon a little pool quite shut off from the main stream, in which a dozen or more frightened minnows were darting about, as if in strange quarters. As I stood watching them and wondering how they got over the dry bar that separated the pool from the river, a kingfisher came sweeping up-stream with a fish in his bill. Seeing me, he whirled silently and disappeared round the point below.

The thought of the curious little wild kindergarten occurred to me suddenly as I turned to the minnows again, and I waded across the river and hid in the bushes. After an hour's wait Koskomenos came stealing back, looked carefully over the pool and the river, and swept down-stream with a rattling call. Presently he came back again with his mate and the whole family; and the little ones, after seeing their parents swoop, and tasting the fish they caught, began to swoop for themselves.

The first plunges were usually in vain, and when a minnow was caught it was undoubtedly one of the wounded fish that Koskomenos had placed there in the lively swarm to encourage his little ones. After a try or two, however, they seemed to get the knack of the thing and would drop like a plummet, bill first, or shoot down on a sharp incline and hit their fish squarely as it darted away into deeper water. The river was wild and difficult, suitable only for expert fishermen. The quietest pools had no fish, and where minnows were found the water or the banks were against the little kingfishers, who had not yet learned to hover and take their fish from the wing. So Koskomenos had found a suitable pool and stocked it himself to make his task of teaching more easy for his mate and more profitable for his little ones. The most interesting point in his method was that, in this case, he had brought the minnows alive to his kindergarten, instead of killing or wounding them, as in the first lesson. He knew that the fish could not get out of the pool, and that his little ones could take their own time in catching them.

When I saw the family again, weeks afterwards, their lessons were well learned; they needed no wounded or captive fish to satisfy their hunger. They were full of the joy of living, and showed me, one day, a curious game, — the only play that I have ever seen among the kingfishers.

There were three of them, when I first found them, perched on projecting stubs over the dancing riffles, which swarmed with chub and " minnies " and samlets and lively young red-fins. Suddenly, as if at the command *go !* they all dropped, bill first, into the river. In a moment they were out again and rushed back to their respective stubs, where they threw their heads back and wriggled their minnows down their throats with a haste to choke them all. That done, they began to dance about on their stubs, clattering and chuckling immoderately.

It was all blind to me at first, till the game was repeated two or three times, always starting at the same instant with a plunge into the riffles and a rush back to goal. Then their object was as clear as the stream below them. With plenty to eat and never a worry in the world, they were playing a game to see which could first get back to his perch and swallow his fish. Sometimes one or two of them failed to get a fish and glided back dejectedly; sometimes all three were so close together that it took a deal of jabber to straighten the matter out; and they always ended in the same way, by beginning all over again.

Koskomenos is a solitary fellow, with few pleasures, and fewer companions to share them with him. This is undoubtedly the result of his peculiar fishing regulations, which give to each kingfisher a certain piece of lake or stream for his own. Only the young of the same family go fishing together; and so I have no doubt that these were the same birds whose early training I had watched, and who were now enjoying themselves in their own way, as all the other Wood Folk do, in the fat, careless, happy autumn days.

PEKOMPF'S
CUNNING

PEKOMPF'S CUNNING

PEKOMPF the wildcat is one of the savage beasts that have not yet vanished from the haunts of men. Sometimes, as you clamber up the wooded hillside above the farm, you will come suddenly upon a fierce-looking, catlike creature stretched out on a rock sunning himself. At sight of you he leaps up with a snarl, and you have a swift instant in which to take his measure. He is twice as big as a house-cat, with round head and big expressionless eyes that glare straight into yours with a hard, greenish glitter. His reddish-brown sides are spotted here and there, and the white fur of his belly is blotched with black — the better to hide himself amid the lights and shadows. A cat, sure enough, but unlike anything of the kind you have ever seen before.

As you look and wonder there is a faint sound that you will do well to heed. The muscles of his long thick legs are working nervously, and under the motion is a warning purr, not the soft rumble in a contented tabby's throat, but the cut and rip of ugly big claws as they are unsheathed viciously upon the dry leaves. His stub tail is twitching — you had not noticed it before, but now it whips back and forth angrily, as if to call attention to the fact that Nature had not altogether forgotten that end of Pekompf. *Whip, whip,* — it *is* a tail — *k'yaaaah!* And you jump as the fierce creature screeches in your face.

If it is your first wildcat, you will hardly know what to do, — to stand perfectly quiet is always best, unless you have a stick or gun in

your hand, — and if you have met Pekompɩ
many times before, you are quite as uncer-
tain what he will do this time. Most wild
creatures, however fierce, prefer to mind their
own business and will respect the same sentiment in you. But when you stumble upon
a wildcat you are never sure of his next
move. That is because he is a slinking,
treacherous creature, like all cats, and never
quite knows how best to meet you. He suspects you unreasonably because he knows
you suspect him with reason. Generally he
slinks away, or leaps suddenly for cover,
according to the method of your approach.
But though smaller he is naturally more savage than either the Canada lynx or the panther, and sometimes he crouches and snarls
in your face, or even jumps for your chest at
the first movement.

Once, to my knowledge, he fell like a fury
upon the shoulders of a man who was hurrying homeward through the twilight, and who
happened to stop unawares under the tree
where Pekompf was watching the runways.
The man had no idea that a wildcat was near,

Pekompf's Cunning

and he probably never would have known had he gone steadily on his way. As he told me afterwards, he felt a sudden alarm and stopped to listen. The moment he did so the savage creature above him thought himself discovered, and leaped to carry the war into Africa. There was a pounce, a screech, a ripping of cloth, a wild yell for help; then the answering shout and rush of two woodsmen with their axes. And that night Pekompf's skin was nailed to the barn-door to dry in the sun before being tanned and made up into a muff for the woodsman's little girl to warm her fingers withal in the bitter winter weather.

Where civilization has driven most of his fellows away, Pekompf is a shy, silent creature; but where the farms are scattered and the hillsides wild and wooded, he is bolder and more noisy than in the unpeopled wilderness. From the door of the charcoal-burner's hut in the Connecticut hills you may still hear him screeching and fighting with his fellows as the twilight falls, and the yowling uproar causes a colder chill in your back than anything you will ever hear in the wilderness.

As you follow the trout stream, from which the charcoal man daily fills his kettle, you may find Pekompf stretched on a fallen log under the alders, glaring intently into the trout pool, waiting, waiting — for what?

Pekompf's Cunning

It will take many seasons of watching to answer this natural question, which every one who is a follower of the wild things has asked himself a score of times. All the cats have but one form of patience, the patience of quiet waiting. Except when hunger-driven, their way of hunting is to watch beside the game paths or crouch upon a big limb above the place where their game comes down to drink. Sometimes they vary their programme by prowling blindly through the woods, singly or in pairs, trusting to luck to blunder upon their game; for they are wretched hunters. They rarely follow a trail, not simply because

Pekompf's Cunning

their noses are not keen — for in the snow, with a trail as plain as a deer path, they break away from it with reckless impatience, only to scare the game into a headlong dash for safety. Then they will crouch under a dwarf spruce and stare at the trail with round unblinking eyes, waiting for the frightened creatures to come back, or for other creatures to come by in the same footprints. Even in teaching her young a mother wildcat is full of snarling whims and tempers; but now let a turkey gobble far away in the woods, let Musquash dive into his den where she can see it, let but a woodmouse whisk out of sight into his hidden doorway, — and instantly patience returns to Pekompf. All the snarling ill-temper vanishes. She crouches and waits, and forgets all else. She may have just fed full on what she likes best, and so have no desire for food and no expectation of catching more; but she must still watch, as if to reassure herself that her eyes are not deceived and that Tookhees is really there under the mossy stone where she saw the scurry of his little legs and heard his frightened squeak as he disappeared.

Pekompf's Cunning

But why should a cat watch at a trout pool, out of which nothing ever comes to reward his patience? That was a puzzling question for many years. I had seen Pekompf many times stretched on a log, or lying close to a great rock over the water, so intent on his watching that he heard not my cautious approach. Twice from my canoe I had seen Upweekis the lynx on the shore of a wilderness lake, crouched among the weather-worn roots of a stranded pine, his great paws almost touching the water, his eyes fixed with unblinking stare on the deep pool below. And once, when trout fishing on a wild river just opposite a great jam of logs and driftwood, I had stopped casting suddenly with an uncanny feeling of being watched by unseen eyes at my solitary sport.

It is always well to heed such a warning in the woods. I looked up and down quickly;

but the river held no life above its hurrying flood. I searched the banks carefully and peered suspiciously into the woods behind me; but save for the dodging of a winter wren, who seems always to be looking for something that he has lost and that he does not want you to know about, the shores were wild and still as if just created. I whipped out my flies again. What was that, just beyond the little wavelet where my Silver Doctor had fallen? Something moved, curled, flipped and twisted nervously. It was a tail, the tip end that cannot be quiet. And there —an irrepressible chill trickled over me as I made out the outlines of a great gray beast stretched on a fallen log, and caught the gleam of

Pekompf's Cunning

his wild eyes fixed steadily upon me. Even as I saw the thing it vanished like a shadow of the woods. But what was the panther watching there before he watched me?

The answer came unexpectedly. It was in the Pemigewasset valley in midsummer. At daybreak I had come softly down the wood road to the trout pool and stopped to watch a mink dodging in and out along the shore. When he passed out of sight under some logs I waited quietly for other Wood Folk to show themselves. A slight move-ment on the end of a log — and there was Pekompf, so still that the eye could hardly find him, stretching a paw down cautiously and flipping it back with a peculiar inward sweep. Again he did it, and I saw the long curved claws, keen as fish-hooks, stretched wide out of their sheaths. He was fishing, spearing his prey with the patience of an Indian; and even as I made the discovery there was a flash of silver following the quick jerk of his paw, and Pekompf leaped to the shore and crouched over the fish that he had thrown out of the water.

Pekompf's Cunning

So Pekompf watches the pools as he watches a squirrel's hole, because he has seen game there and because he likes fish above everything else that the woods can furnish. But how often must he watch the big trout before he catches one? Sometimes, in the late twilight, the largest fish will move out of the pools and nose along the shore for food, their back fins showing out of the shallow water as they glide along. It may be that Pekompf sometimes catches them at this time, and so when he sees the gleam of a fish in the depths he crouches where he is for a while, following the irresistible impulse of all cats at the sight of game. Herein they differ from all other savage beasts, which, when not hungry, pay no attention whatever to smaller animals.

It may be, also, that Pekompf's cunning is deeper than this. Old Noel, a Micmac hunter, tells me that both wildcat and lynx, whose cunning is generally the cunning of stupidity, have discovered a remarkable way of catching fish. They will lie with their heads close to the water, their paws curved for a quick

" A flash of silver following the quick
jerk of his paw "

grab, their eyes half shut to deceive the fish, and their whiskers just touching and playing with the surface. Their general color blends with that of their surroundings and hides them perfectly. The trout, noticing the slight crinkling of the water where the long whiskers touch it, but not separating the crouching animal from the log or rock on which he rests, rise to the surface, as is their wont when feeding, and are snapped out by a lightning sweep of the paws.

Whether this be so or not I am not sure. The raccoon undoubtedly catches crabs and little fish in this way; and I have sometimes surprised cats — both wildcats and Canada lynxes, as well as domestic tabbies — with their heads down close to the water, so still that they seemed part of the log or rock on which they crouched. Once I tried for five minutes to make a guide see a big lynx that was lying on a root in plain sight within thirty yards of our canoe, while the guide assured me in a whisper that he could see perfectly and that it was only a stump. Then, hearing us, the lynx rose, stared, and leaped for the brush.

Pekompf's Cunning

Pekompf's Cunning

Such hiding would easily deceive even a trout, for I have often taken my position at the edge of a jam and after lying perfectly still for ten minutes have seen the wary fish rise from under the logs to investigate a straw or twig that I held in my fingers and with which I touched the water here and there, like an insect at play.

So Old Noel is probably right when he says that Pekompf fishes with his whiskers, for the habits of both fish and cats seem to carry out his observations.

But deeper than his cunning is Pekompf's inborn suspicion and his insane fury at being opposed or cornered. The trappers catch him, as they catch his big cousin the lucivee, by setting a snare in the rabbit paths that he nightly follows. Opposite the noose and attached to the other end of the cord is a pole, which jumps after the cat as he starts forward with the loop about his neck. Were it a fox, now, he would back away out of the snare, or lie still and cut the cord with his teeth and so escape. But, like all cats when trapped, Pekompf flies into a blind fury. He screeches at the unoffending stick, claws it, battles with it, and literally chokes himself in his rage. Or, if he be an old cat and his cunning a bit deeper, he will go off cautiously and climb the biggest tree he can find, with the uncomfortable thing that he is tied to dangling and clattering behind him. When near the top he will leave the stick hanging on one side of a limb while he cunningly climbs down the other, thinking thus to fool his dumb enemy and leave him behind. One of two things always happens. Either the stick catches in the crotch and Pekompf hangs himself on his own gibbet, or else it comes over with a sudden jerk and falls to the ground, pulling Pekompf with it and generally killing him in the fall.

It is a cruel, brutal kind of device at best, and fortunately for the cat tribe has almost vanished from the northern woods, except in

Pekompf's Cunning

Pekompf's Cunning

the far Northwest, where the half-breeds still use it for lynx successfully. But as a study of the way in which trappers seize upon some peculiarity of an animal and use it for his destruction, it has no equal.

That Pekompf's cunning is of the cat kind, suspicious without being crafty or intelligent like that of the fox or wolf, is curiously shown by a habit which both lynx and wild-cat have in common, namely, that of carrying anything they steal to the top of some lofty evergreen to devour it. When they catch a rabbit or fish fairly themselves, they generally eat it on the spot; but when they steal the same animal from snare or *cache*, or from some smaller hunter, the cat suspicion returns — together with some dim sense of wrong-doing, which all animals feel more or less — and they make off with the booty and eat it greedily where they think no one will ever find them.

Once, when watching for days under a fish-hawk's nest to see the animals that came in shyly to eat the scraps that the little fish-hawks cast out when their hunger was satis-fied, this cat habit was strikingly manifest. Other animals would come in and quietly eat what they found and slip away again; but the cats would seize on a morsel with flash-ing eyes, as if defying all law and order, and would either growl horribly as they ate or else would slink away guiltily and, as I found out by following, would climb the biggest tree at hand and eat the morsel in the high-est crotch that gave a foothold. And once, on the Maine coast in November, I saw a fierce battle in the tree-tops where a wildcat crouched, snarling like twenty fiends, while a big eagle whirled and swooped over him, trying to take away the game that Pekompf had stolen.

By far the most curious bit of Pekompf's cunning came under my eyes, one summer, a few years ago. Until recently I had sup-posed it to be a unique discovery; but last summer a friend, who goes to Newfoundland every year for the salmon fishing, had a simi-lar experience with a Canada lynx, which

Pekompf's Cunning

emphasizes the tendency of all cats to seek the tree-tops with anything that they have stolen; though curiously enough I have never found any trace of it with game that they had caught honestly themselves. It was in Nova Scotia, where I was trout fishing for a little season, and where I had no idea of meeting Pekompf, for the winters are severe there and the wildcat is supposed to leave such places to his more powerful and longer-legged cousin, the lynx, whose feet are bigger than his and better padded for walking on the snow. Even in the southern Berkshires you may follow Pekompf's trail and see where he makes heavy weather of it, floundering belly-deep like a domestic tabby through the soft drifts in his hungry search for grouse and rabbits, and lying down in despair at last to wait till the snow settles. But to my surprise Pekompf was there, bigger, fiercer, and more cunning than I had ever seen him; though I did not discover this till after a long search.

I had fished from dawn till almost six

o'clock, one morning, and had taken two good trout, which were all that the stream promised to yield for the day. Then I thought of a little pond in the woods over the mountain, which looked trouty when I had discovered it and which, so far as I knew, had never been fished with a fly. Led more by the fun of exploring than by the expectation of fish, I started to try the new waters.

Pekompf's Cunning

The climb through the woods promised to be a hard one, so I left everything behind except rod, reel, and fly-book. My coat was hung on the nearest bush; the landing-net lay in the shade across a rock, the end of the handle wedged under a root, and I dropped my two trout into that and covered them from the sun with ferns and moss. Then I started off through the woods for the little pond.

When I came back empty-handed, a few hours later, trout and landing-net were gone. The first thought naturally was that some one had stolen them, and I looked for the thief's tracks; but, save my own, there was not a footprint anywhere beside the stream up or down. Then I looked beside the rock more carefully and found bits of moss and fish-scales, and the pugs of some animal, too faint in the gravel to make out what the beast was that made them. I followed the faint traces for a hundred yards or more into the woods till they led me to a great spruce tree, under which every sign disappeared utterly, as if the creature had suddenly flown away net and all, and I gave up the trail without any idea of what had made it.

For two weeks that theft bothered me. It was not so much the loss of my two trout and net, but rather the loss of my woodcraft on the trail that had no end, which kept me restless. The net was a large one, altogether too large and heavy for trout fishing. At the last moment before starting on my trip I found that my trout net was rotten and useless, and so had taken the only thing at hand, a specially made forty-inch net which I had last used on a scientific expedition for collecting specimens from the lakes of northern New Brunswick. The handle was long, and the bow, as I had more than once tested, was powerful enough to use instead of a gaff for taking a twenty-five pound salmon out of his pool after he had been played to a standstill; and how any creature could drag it off through the woods without leaving a plain trail for my eyes to follow puzzled me, and excited a most lively curiosity to know who he was and why he had not eaten the fish where he found them. Was it lynx or stray wolf, or had the terrible Injun Devil that is still spoken of with awe at the winter firesides returned to his native woods? For a week I puzzled over the question; then I went back to the spot and tried in vain to follow the faint marks in the moss. After that whenever I wandered near the spot I tried the trail again, or circled wider and wider through the woods, hoping to find the net or some positive sign of the beast that had stolen it.

One day in the woods it occurred to me suddenly that, while I had followed the trail three or four times, I had never thought to examine the tree beneath which it ended. At the thought

213

Pekompf's Cunning

I went to the big spruce and there, sure enough, were flecks of bright brown here and there where the rough outer shell had been chipped off. And there also, glimmering white, was a bit of dried slime where a fish had rested for an instant against the bark. The beast, whatever he was, had climbed the tree with his booty; and the discovery was no sooner made than I was shinning up eagerly after him.

Near the scraggy top I found my net, its long handle wedged firmly in between two branches, its bow caught on a projecting stub, its bag hanging down over empty space. In the net was a big wildcat, his round head driven through a hole which he had bitten in the bottom, the tough meshes drawn taut as fiddle-strings about his throat. All four legs had clawed or pushed their way through the mesh, till every kick and struggle served only to bind and choke him more effectually.

From marks I made out at last the outline of the story. Pekompf had found the fish and tried to steal them, but his suspicions were roused by the queer net and the clattering handle. With true lynx cunning, which is always more than half stupidity, he had carried it off and started to climb the biggest tree he could find. Near the top the handle had wedged among the branches, and while he tried to dislodge it net and fish had swung clear of the trunk. In the bark below the handle I found where he had clung to the tree boll and tried to reach the swinging trout with his paw; and on a branch above the bow were marks which showed where he had looked down longingly at the fish at the bottom of the net, just below his hungry nose. From this branch he had either fallen or, more likely, in a fit of blind rage had leaped into the net, which closed around him and held him more effectually than bars of iron. When I came under the tree for the first time, following his trail, he was probably crouched on a limb over my head watching me steadily; and when I came back the second time he was dead.

That was all that one could be sure about. But here and there, in a torn

215

Pekompf's Cunning

Pekompf's Cunning

mesh, or a tuft of fur, or the rip of a claw against a swaying twig, were the marks of a struggle whose savage intensity one could only imagine.

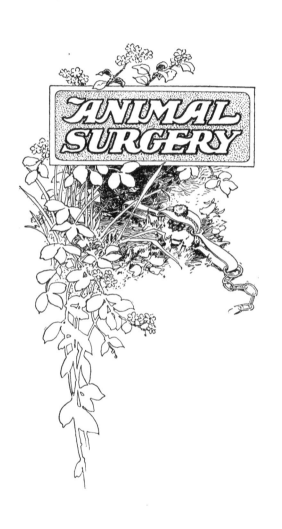

ANIMAL SURGERY

ANIMAL SURGERY

MOST people have seen a sick cat eat grass, or an uneasy dog seek out some weed and devour it greedily to make his complaining stomach feel better. Some few may have read John Wesley's directions on the art of keeping well — which have not, however, found their way into his book of discipline for the soul — and have noted with surprised interest his claim that many medicines in use among the common people and the physicians of his time were discovered by watching the animals that sought out these things to heal their diseases. " If they heal animals they will also heal men," is his invincible argument. Others may have dipped deep into Indian history and folk-lore and learned that many of the herbs used by the American tribes, and especially the cures for rheumatism, dysentery, fever, and snake bites, were learned direct from the animals, by noting the rheumatic old bear grub for fern roots or bathe in the hot mud of a sulphur spring, and by watching with eager eyes what plants the wild creatures ate when bitten by rattlers or wasted by the fever. Still others have been fascinated with the first crude medical knowledge of the Greeks, which came to them from the East undoubtedly, and have read that the guarded mysteries of the Asclepiades, the healing cult that followed Æsculapius, had among them many simple remedies that had first proved their efficacy among animals in a natural state; and that Hippocrates, the greatest physician of antiquity, whose fame under the name of Bokrat the Wise went down through Arabia and into the farthest deserts, owes many of his medical aphorisms

"Escaped at last by swimming
an icy river"

to what he himself, or his forebears, must
have seen out of doors among the wild
creatures. And all these seers and readers
have perhaps wondered how much the animals knew, and especially how they came to
know it.

To illustrate the matter simply and in our
own day and generation: A deer that has
been chased all day long by dogs, and that
has escaped at last by swimming an icy river
and fallen exhausted on the farther shore,
will lie down to sleep in the snow. That
would mean swift death for any human
being. Half the night the deer will move
about at short intervals, instead of sleeping
heavily, and in the morning he is as good
as ever and ready for another run. The
same deer shut up in a warm barn to sleep
overnight, as has been more than once
tested with park animals, will be found dead
in the morning.

Here is a natural law of healing suggested,
which, if noted among the Greeks and Indians, would have been adopted instantly as
a method of dealing with extreme cold and

exhaustion, or with poisoning resulting in pa-
ralysis of the muscles. Certainly the method,
if somewhat crude, might still have wrought
enough cures to be looked upon with venera-
tion by a people who unfortunately had no
knowledge of chemical drugs, or Scotch
whisky, or sugar pellets with an ethereal
suggestion of intangible triturations somewhere in the midst of them.

That the animals do practice at times a
rude kind of medicine and surgery upon
themselves is undeniable. The only question about it is, How do they know? To
say it is a matter of instinct is but begging
the question. It is also three-fourths fool-
ishness, for many of the things that animals
do are beyond the farthest scope of instinct.
The case of the deer that moved about and
so saved his life, instead of sleeping on
heavily to his death, may be partly a case
of instinct. Personally it seems to me more
a matter of experience;
for a fawn under the
same circumstances,
unless his mother were

near to keep him moving, would undoubtedly
lie down and die.   More than that, it seems
to be largely a matter of obedience to the
strongest impulse of the moment, to which
all animals are accustomed or trained from
their birthday.   And that is not quite the
same thing as instinct, unless one is disposed
to go to the extreme of Berkeley's philosophy
and make instinct a kind of spirit-personality
that watches over animals all the time.   Often
the knowledge of healing or of primitive surgery seems to be the discovery or possession
of a few rare individual animals, instead of
being spread widecast among the species, as
instincts are.   This knowledge, or what-you-
may-call-it, is sometimes shared, and so hints
at a kind of communication among animals,
of whose method we catch only fleeting
glimpses and suggestions — but that will be
the subject of another article.   The object
of this is, not to answer the questions of
how or whence, but simply to suggest one
or two things I have seen in the woods
as the basis for further and more detailed
observations.

The most elemental kind of surgery is that which amputates a leg when it is broken, not always or often, but only when the wound festers from decay or fly-bite and so endangers the whole body. Probably the best illustration of this is found in the coon, who has a score of traits that place him very high among intelligent animals. When a coon's foot is shattered by a bullet he will cut it off promptly and wash the stump in running water, partly to reduce the inflammation and partly, no doubt, to make it perfectly clean. As it heals he uses his tongue on the wound freely, as a dog does, to cleanse it perhaps, and by the soft massage of his tongue to reduce the swelling and allay the pain.

So far this may or may not be pure instinct. For I do not know, and who will tell me, whether a child puts his wounded hand to his mouth and sucks and cleanses the hurt by pure instinct, or because he has seen others do it, or because he has had his hurts kissed away in childhood, and so imitates the action unconsciously when his mother is not near?

Most mother animals tongue their little ones freely. Now is that a caress, or is it some hygienic measure begun at birth, when she devours all traces of the birth-envelopes and licks the little ones clean lest the nose of some hungry prowler bring him near to destroy the family? Certainly the young are conscious of the soft tongue that rubs them fondly, and so when they lick their own wounds it may be only a memory and an imitation,—two factors, by the way, which lie at the bottom of all elemental education. That explanation, of course, leaves the amputated leg out of the question; and the surgery does not stop here.

When a boy, and still barbarian enough to delight in trapping, partly from a love of the chase that was born in me, and partly to put money into a boy's empty pocket, I once caught a muskrat in a steel trap that slid off into deep water at the first pull and so drowned the creature mercifully. This was due to the careful instructions of Natty Dingle, at whose feet I sat to learn woodcraft, and who used the method to save all

Animal Surgery

his pelts; for often an animal, when caught in a trap, will snap the bone by a twist of his body and then cut the leg off with his teeth, and so escape, leaving his foot in the trap's jaws. This is common enough among fur-bearing animals to excite no comment; and it is sad now to remember that sometimes I would find animals drowned in my traps, that had previously suffered at the hands of other trappers.

I remember especially one big musquash that I was going to shoot near one of my traps, when I stopped short at noticing some queer thing about him. The trap was set in shallow water where a path made by muskrats came up out of the river into the grass. Just over the trap was a turnip on a pointed stick to draw the creature's attention and give him something to anticipate until he should put his foot on the deadly pan beneath. But the old musquash avoided the path, as if he had suffered in such places before. Instead of following the ways of his ancestors he came out at another spot behind the trap, and I saw with horrible regret that he had cut off both his fore legs, probably at different times, when he had been twice caught in man's abominable inventions. When he came up out of the stream he rose on his hind legs and waddled through the grass like a bear or a monkey, for he had no fore feet to rest upon. He climbed a tussock beside the bait with immense caution, pulled in the turnip with his two poor stumps of forearms, ate it where he was, and slipped back into the stream again; while the boy watched with a new wonder in the twilight, and forgot all about the gun as he tended his traps.

It does not belong with my story, but that night the traps came in, and never went out again; and I can never pass a trap now anywhere without poking a stick into it to save some poor innocent leg.

All this is digression; and I have almost forgotten my surgery and the particular muskrat I was talking about. He, too, had been caught in some other fellow's trap and had bitten his leg off only a few days before. The wound was not yet healed, and the amazing thing about it was that he had covered it with some kind of sticky vegetable gum, probably from some pine-tree that had been split or barked close to the ground where Musquash could reach it easily. He had smeared it thickly all over the wound and well up the leg above it, so that all dirt and even all air and water were excluded perfectly.

An old Indian who lives and hunts on Vancouver Island told me recently that he has several times caught beaver that had previously cut their legs off to escape from traps, and that two of them had covered the wounds thickly with gum, as the muskrat had done. Last spring the same Indian caught a bear in a deadfall. On the animal's side was a long rip from some other bear's claw, and the wound had been smeared thickly with soft spruce resin. This last experience corresponds closely with one of my own. I shot a big bear, years ago, in northern New Brunswick, that had received a gunshot wound, which had raked him badly and then penetrated the leg. He had plugged the wound carefully with clay,

evidently to stop the bleeding, and then had
covered the broken skin with sticky mud
from the river's brink, to keep the flies away
from the wound and give it a chance to heal
undisturbed. It is noteworthy here that the
bear uses either gum or clay indifferently,
while the beaver and muskrat seem to know
enough to avoid the clay, which would be
quickly washed off in the water.

Here are a few incidents, out of a score
or more that I have seen, or heard from reli-
able hunters, that indicate something more
than native instinct among animals. When
I turn to the birds the incidents are fewer
but more remarkable; for the birds, being
lower in the scale of life, are more subject
to instinct than are the animals, and so are
less easily taught by their mothers, and are
slower to change their natural habits to meet
changing conditions.

This is, of course, a very general state-
ment and is subject to endless exceptions.
The finches that, when transported to Aus-
tralia from England, changed the style of
their nests radically and now build in a

fashion entirely different from that of their parents; the little goldfinch of New England that will build a false bottom to her nest to cover up the egg of a cow-bird that has been left to hatch among her own; the grouse that near the dwellings of men are so much wilder and keener than their brethren of the wilderness; the swallows that adopt the chimneys and barns of civilization instead of the hollow trees and clay banks of their native woods, — all these and a score of others show how readily instinct is modified among the birds, and how the young are taught a wisdom that their forefathers never knew. Nevertheless it is true, I think, that instincts are generally sharper with them than with animals, and the following cases suggest all the more strongly that we must look beyond instinct to training and individual discovery to account for many things among the feathered folk.

The most wonderful bit of bird surgery that has ever come to my attention is that of the woodcock that set his broken leg in a clay cast, as related in a previous chapter;

but there is one other almost as remarkable
that opens up a question that is even harder
to answer. One day in the early spring I
saw two eider-ducks swimming about the
Hummock Pond on the island of Nantucket.
The keen-eyed critic will interfere here and
say I was mistaken; for eiders are salt-water
ducks that haunt only the open sea and are
supposed never to enter fresh water, not
even to breed. That is what I also supposed until I saw these two; so I sat down
to watch a while and find out, if possible,
what had caused them to change their
habits. At this time of year the birds are
almost invariably found in pairs, and sometimes a flock a hundred yards long will pass
you, flying close to the water and sweeping
around the point where you are watching,
first a pretty brown female and then a gor-
geous black-and-white drake just behind her,
alternating with perfect regularity, female and
male, throughout the whole length of the
long line. The two birds before me, however,
were both females; and
that was another reason

for watching them instead of the hundreds of other ducks, coots and sheldrakes and broadbills that were scattered all over the big pond.

The first thing noticed was that the birds were acting queerly, dipping their heads under water and keeping them there for a full minute or more at a time. That was also curious, for the water under them was too deep for feeding, and the eiders prefer to wait till the tide falls and then gather the exposed shellfish from the rocks, rather than to dive after them like a coot. Darkness came on speedily to hide the birds, who were still dipping their heads as if bewitched, and I went away no wiser for my watching.

A few weeks later there was another eider, a big drake, in the same pond, behaving in the same queer way. Thinking perhaps that this was a wounded bird that had gone crazy from a shot in the head, I pushed out after him in an old tub of a boat; but he took wing at my approach, like any other duck, and after a vigorous flight lit farther down the pond and plunged his head under water again. Thoroughly curious now, I went on a still hunt after the stranger, and after much difficulty succeeded in shooting him from the end of a bushy point. The only unusual thing about him was that a large mussel, such as grow on the rocks in salt water, had closed his shells firmly on the bird's tongue in such a way that he could neither be crushed by the bird's bill nor scratched off by the bird's foot. I pulled the mussel off, put it in my pocket, and went home more mystified than before.

That night I hunted up an old fisherman, who had a big store of information in his head about all kinds of wild things, and asked him if he had ever seen a shoal-duck in fresh water. "Once or twice," he said; "they kept dipping their heads under water, kinder crazy like." But he had no explanation to offer until I showed him the mussel that I had found on the duck's tongue. Then his face lightened. "Mussels of that kind won't live in fresh water," he declared at a glance; and then the explanation of the birds' queer actions flashed into both our heads at once: the eiders were simply drowning the mussels in order to make them loosen their grip and release the captive tongues.

This is undoubtedly the true explanation, as I made sure by testing the mussels in fresh water and by watching the birds more closely at their feeding. All winter they may be found along our coasts, where they feed on the small shellfish that cover the ledges. As the tide goes down they swim in from the shoals, where they rest in scattered flocks, and chip the mussels from the ledges, swallowing them shells and all. A score of times I have hidden among the rocks of the jetty with a few wooden decoys in front of me, and watched the eiders come in to feed. They would approach the decoys rapidly, lifting their wings repeatedly as a kind of salutation; then, angered apparently that they were not welcomed by the same signal of uplifted wings, they would swim up to the wooden frauds and peck them savagely here and there, and then leave them in disgust and scatter among the rocks at my feet, paying little attention to me as long as I kept perfectly still. For they are much tamer than other wild ducks, and are, unfortunately, slow to believe that man is their enemy.

I noticed another curious thing while watching them and hoping that by some chance I might see one caught by a mussel. When a flock was passing high overhead, any sudden noise — a shout, or the near report of a gun — would make the whole flock swoop down like a flash close to the water. Plover have the same habit when they first arrive from Labrador, but I have hunted in vain for any satisfactory explanation of the thing.

As the birds feed a mussel will sometimes close his shells hard on some careless duck's tongue or bill in such a way that he cannot be crushed or swallowed or broken against the rocks. In that case the bird, if he knows the secret, will fly to fresh water and drown his tormentor. Whether all the ducks have this wisdom, or whether it is confined to a few rare birds, there is no present means of knowing. I have seen three different eiders practice this bit of surgery myself, and have heard of at least a dozen more, all of the same species, that were seen in fresh ponds or rivers, dipping their heads under water repeatedly. In either case two interesting questions suggest themselves: first, How did a bird whose whole life from birth to death is spent on the sea first learn that certain mussels will drown in fresh water? and, second, How do the other birds know it now, when the need arises unexpectedly?

HUNTING WITHOUT A GUN

Hunting Without a Gun

THE man who hunts with gun or camera has his reward. He has also his labors, vexations, and failures; and these are the price he pays for his success. The man who hunts without either gun or camera has, it seems to me, a much greater reward, and has it without price. Of him more than any other Nimrod may be said what a returned missionary from Africa said of his first congregation, "They are a contented folk, clothed

Hunting Without a Gun

with the sunlight and fed by gravitation." Hunting without a gun is, therefore, the sport of a peaceful man, a man who goes to the woods for rest and for letting his soul grow, and who after a year of worry and work is glad to get along without either for a little season. As he glides over the waterways in his canoe, or loafs leisurely along the trail, he carries no weight of gun or tripod or extra plates. Glad to be alive himself, he has no pleasure in the death of the wild things. Content just to see and hear and understand, he has no fret or sweat to get the sun just right and calculate his exact thirty-foot distance and then to fume and swear, as I have heard good men do, because the game fidgets, or the clouds obscure the sun, or the plates are not quick enough, or — beginning of sorrows! — because he finds after the game has fled that the film he has just used on a bull moose had all its good qualities already preëmpted by a landscape and a passing canoe.

I have no desire to decry any kind of legitimate hunting, for I have tried them all and

" The bear and her cubs are gathering blueberries
in their greedy, funny way "

the rewards are good. I simply like hunting without a gun or camera better than all other forms of hunting for three good reasons: first, because it is lazy and satisfying, perfect for summer weather; second, because it has no troubles, no vexations, no disappointments, and so is good for a man who has wrestled long enough with these things; and third, because it lets you into the life and individuality of the wild animals as no other hunting can possibly do, since you approach them with a mind at ease and, having no excitement about you, they dare to show themselves natural and unconcerned, or even a bit curious about you to know who you are and what you are doing. It has its thrills and excitements too, as much or as little as you like. To creep up through the brûlée to where the bear and her cubs are gathering blueberries in their greedy, funny way; to paddle silently upon a big moose while his head is under water and only his broad antlers show; to lie at ease beside the trail flecked with sunlight and shadow and have the squirrels scamper across your legs, or the

wild bird perch inquisitively upon your toe, or — rarest sight in the woods in the early morning — to have a fisher twist by you in intense, weasel-like excitement, puzzling out the trail of the hare or grouse that passed you an hour ago; to steal along the waterways alone on a still dark night and open your jack silently upon ducks or moose or mother deer and her fawns, — there is joy and tingle enough in all these things to satisfy any lover of the woods. There is also wisdom to be found, especially when you remember that these are individual animals that no human eyes have ever before looked upon, that they are different every one, and that at any moment they may reveal some queer trick or trait of animal life that no naturalist has ever before seen.

Last summer, just below my camp on Matagammon, was a little beach between two points surrounded by dense woods that *Hunting* the deer seemed to love better than any *Without a Gun* other spot on the whole lake. When we first arrived the deer were close about our camp. From the door we could sometimes see them on the lake shore, and every evening at twilight they would steal up shyly to eat the potato and apple parings. Gradually the noises of camp drove them far back on the ridges, though on stormy nights they would come back when the camp was still and all lights out. From my tent I would hear cautious rustlings or the crack of a twig above the drip and pour of raindrops on my tent-fly, and stealing out in the darkness would find two or three deer, generally a doe and her fawns, standing under the split roof of our woodshed to escape the pelting rain.

The little beach was farther away, across an arm of the lake and out of sight and sound of our camp, so the deer never deserted it, though we watched them there every day. Just why they liked it I could never discover.

A score of beaches on the lake were larger and smoother, and a dozen at least offered better feeding; but the deer came here in greater numbers than anywhere else. Near-by was a great wild meadow, with dense hiding-places on the slopes beyond, where deer were numerous. Before the evening feeding began in the wild meadow they would come out to this little beach and play for an hour or so; and I have no doubt the place was a regular playground, such as rabbits and foxes and crows, and indeed most wild animals, choose for their hours of fun.

Once, at early twilight, I lay in hiding among some old roots at the end of this little beach, watching a curious game. Eight or ten deer, does and fawns and young spike bucks, had come out into the open and were now running rapidly in three circles arranged in a line, so, o○o. In the middle was a big circle some fifteen feet in diameter, and at opposite sides were two smaller circles less than half the diameter of the first, as I found afterwards by measuring from the tracks. Around one of these small circles the deer

ran from right to left invariably; around the
other they ran from left to right; and around
the big middle circle they ran either way,
though when two or three were running this
circle together, while the others bounded
about the ends, they all ran the same way.
As they played, all the rings were in use at
once, the two small end rings being much
more used than the big one. The individual
deer passed rapidly from one ring to the
others, but — and here is the queerest part
of it all — I did not see a single deer, not
even one of the fawns, cut across the
big circle from one end ring to the
other. After they were gone the rings
showed clearly in
the sand, but not
a single track led
across any of the
circles.

The object of
the play was sim-
ple enough. Aside
from the fun, the
young deer were

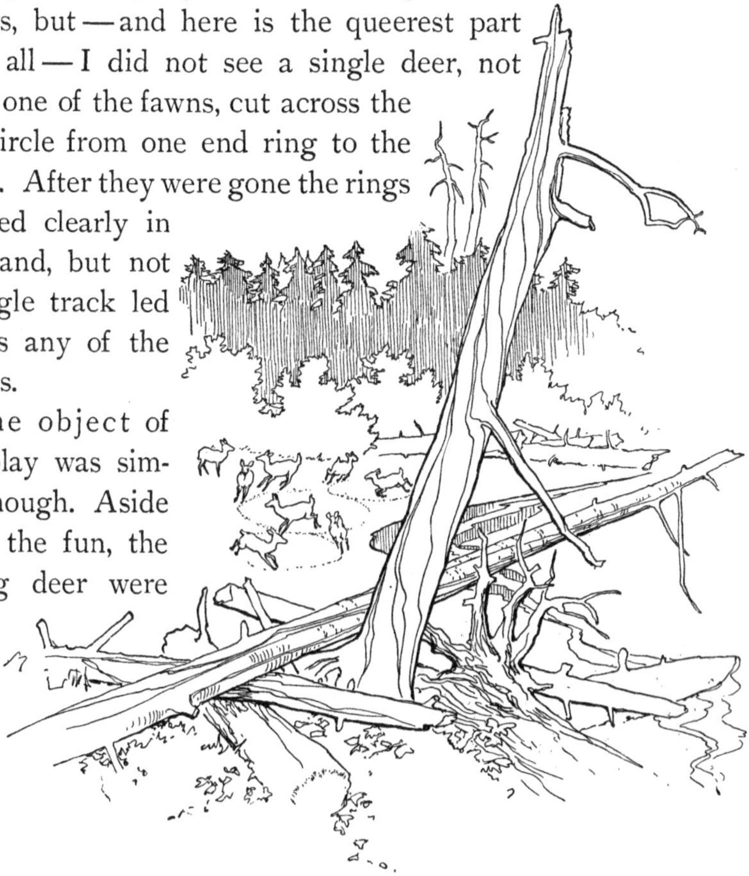

being taught to twist and double quickly; but what the rules of the game were, and whether they ran in opposite circles to avoid getting dizzy, was more than I could discover, though the deer were never more than thirty yards away from me and I could watch every move clearly without my field-glasses. That the game and some definite way of playing it were well understood by the deer no one could doubt who watched this wonderful play for five minutes. Though they ran swiftly, with astonishing lightness and grace, there was no confusion. Every now and then one of the does would leap forward and head off one of her fawns as he headed into the big ring, when like a flash he would whirl in his tracks and away with a *bl-r-r-t!* of triumph or dissatisfaction. Once a spike buck, and again a doe with two well-grown fawns, trotted out of the woods and, after watching the dizzy play for a moment, leaped into it as if they under-

stood perfectly what was expected. They played this game only for a few minutes at a time; then they would scatter and move up and down the shore leisurely and nose the water. Soon one or two would come back, and in a moment the game would be in full swing again, the others joining it swiftly as the little creatures whirled about the rings, exercising every muscle and learning how to control their graceful bodies perfectly, though they had no idea that older heads had planned the game for them with a purpose.

Watching them thus at their play, the meaning of a curious bit of deer anatomy became clear. A deer's shoulder is not attached to the skeleton at all; it lies loosely inside the skin, with only a bit of delicate elastic tissue joining it to the muscles of the body. When a deer was headed suddenly and braced himself in his tracks, the body would lunge forward till the fore legs seemed hung almost in the middle of his belly. Again, when he kicked up his heels, they would seem to be supporting his neck, far forward of where they properly belonged. This free action of the shoulder is what gives the wonderful flexibility and grace to a deer's movements, just as it takes and softens all

the shock of falling in his high-jumping run among the rocks and over the endless windfalls of the wilderness.

In the midst of the play, and after I had watched it for a full half-hour, there was a swift rustle in the woods on my right, and I caught my breath sharply at sight of a magnificent buck standing half hid in the underbrush. There were two or three big bucks with splendid antlers that lived lazily on the slopes above this part of the lake, and that I had been watching and following for several weeks. Unlike the does and fawns and young bucks, they were wild as hawks and selfish as cats. They rarely showed themselves in the open, and if surprised there with other deer they bounded away at the first sight or sniff of danger. Does and little fawns, when they saw you, would instantly stamp and whistle to warn the other deer before they had taken the first step to save themselves or investigate the danger; but the big bucks would bound or glide away, according to the method of your approach, and in saving their own skins, as they thought, would have absolutely no concern for the safety of the herd feeding near by. — And that is one reason why, in a natural state, deer rarely allow the bucks and bulls to lead them.

The summer laziness was still upon these big bucks; the wild fall running had not seized them. Once I saw a curious and canny bit of their laziness. I had gone off with a guide to try the trout at a distant lake. While I watched a porcupine and tried to win his confidence with sweet chocolate — a bad shot, by the way — the guide went on far ahead. As he climbed a ridge, busy with thoughts of the dim blazed trail he was following, I noticed a faint stir in some bushes on one side, and through my glass I made out the head of a big buck that was watching the guide keenly from his hiding. It was in the late forenoon, when deer are mostly resting, and the lazy buck was debating, probably, w h e t h e r it were necessary for him to run or not. The guide passed

rapidly; then to my astonishment the head disappeared as the buck lay down where he was.

Keeping my eyes on the spot, I followed on the guide's trail. There was no sign of life in the thicket as I passed, though beyond a doubt the wary old buck was watching my every motion keenly. When I had gone well past and still the thicket remained all quiet, I turned gradually and walked towards it. There was a slight rustle as the buck rose to his feet again. He had evidently planned for me to follow the steps of the other man, and had not thought it worth while to stand up. Another slow step or two on my part, then another rustle and a faint motion of underbrush — so faint that, had there been a wind blowing, my eye would scarcely have noticed it — told me where the buck had glided away silently to another covert, where he turned and stood to find out whether I had discovered him, or whether my change of direction had any other motive than the natural wandering of a man lost in the woods.

That was far back on the ridges, where most of the big bucks loaf and hide, each one by himself, during the summer. Down at the lake, however, there were two or three that for some reason occasionally showed themselves with the other deer, but were so shy and wild that hunting them without a gun was almost impossible. It was one of these big fellows that now stood half hid in the underbrush within twenty yards of me, watching the deer's game impatiently.

A stamp of his foot and a low snort stopped the play instantly, and the big buck moved out on the shore in full view. He looked out over the lake, where he had so often seen the canoes of men moving; his nose tried the wind up shore; eyes and ears searched below, where I was lying; then he scanned the lake again keenly. Perhaps he had seen my canoe upturned among the water-grasses far away; more probably it was the unknown sense or *feel* of an enemy, which they who hunt with or without a gun find so often among the larger wild animals, that made him restless and suspicious. While he watched and searched the lake and the shores not a deer stirred from his tracks. Some command was in the air which I myself seemed to feel in my hiding. Suddenly the big buck turned and glided away into the woods, and every deer on the shore followed instantly without question or hesitation. Even the little fawns, never so heedless as to miss a signal, felt something in the buck's attitude deeper than their play, something perhaps in the air that was not noticed before, and trotted after their mothers, fading away at last like shadows into the darkening woods.

On another lake, years before, when hunting in the same way without a gun, I saw another curious bit of deer wisdom. It must be remembered that deer are born apparently without any fear of man. The fawns when found very young in the woods are generally full of playfulness and curiosity; and a fawn that has lost its mother will turn to a man quicker than to any other animal. When deer see you for the first time, no matter how old or young they are, they approach cautiously, if you do not terrify them by sudden motions, and in twenty pretty ways try to find out what you are. Like most wild animals that have a keen sense of smell, and especially like the bear and caribou, they trust only their noses at first. When they scent man for the first time they generally run away, not because they know what it means but for precisely the opposite reason, namely, because there is in the air a strong scent that they do not know, and that they have not been taught by their mothers how to meet. When in doubt run away — that is the rule of nose which seems to be impressed by their mothers upon all timid wild things, though they act in almost the opposite way when sight or hearing is in question.

All this is well known to hunters; but now comes the curious exception. After I had been watching the deer for some weeks at one of their playgrounds, a guide came into camp with his wife and little child. They were on their way in to their own camp for the hunting season. To please

the little one, who was fond of all animals, I took her with me to show her the deer playing. As they were running about on the shore I sent her out of our hiding, in a sudden spirit of curiosity, to see what the deer and fawns would do. True to her instructions, the little one walked out very slowly into the midst of them. They started at first; two of the old deer circled down instantly to wind her; but even after getting her scent, the suspicious man-scent that most of them had been taught to fear, they approached fearlessly, their ears set forward, and their expressive tails down without any of the nervous wiggling that is so manifest whenever their owners catch the first suspicious smell in the air. The child, meanwhile, sat on the shore, watching the pretty creatures with wide-eyed curiosity, but obeying my first whispered instructions like a little hero and keeping still as a hunted rabbit. Two little spotted fawns were already circling about her playfully, but the third went straight up to her, stretching his nose and ears forward to show his friendliness, and then drawing back to

stamp his little fore foot prettily to make the
silent child move or speak, and perhaps also
to show her in deer fashion that, though
friendly, he was not at all afraid.

There was one buck in the group, a three-
year-old with promising antlers. At first he
was the only deer that showed any fear of
the little visitor; and his fear seemed to me
to be largely a matter of suspicion, or of irri-
tation that anything should take away the
herd's attention from himself. The fall wildness was coming upon him, and he showed
it by restless fidgeting, by frequent proddings
of the does with his antlers, and by driving
them about roughly and unreasonably. Now
he approached the child with a shake of his
antlers, not to threaten her, it seemed to me,
but rather to show the other deer that he was
still master, the Great Mogul who
must be consulted upon all occasions. For the first
time the little girl
started nervously at the
threatening motion. I
called softly to her to

keep still and not be afraid, at the same time rising up quietly from my hiding-place. Instantly the little comedy changed as the deer whirled in my direction. They had seen men before and knew what it meant. The white flags flew up over the startled backs, and the air fairly bristled with whistling *h-e-e-e-yeu*, *he-u's* as deer and fawns rose over the nearest windfalls like a flock of frightened partridges and plunged away into the shelter of the friendly woods.

There are those who claim that the life of an animal is a mere matter of blind instinct and habit. Here on the shore before my eyes was a scene that requires a somewhat different explanation.

Though deer are the most numerous and the most interesting animals to be hunted without a gun, they are by no means the only game to fill the hunter's heart full and make him glad that his game bag is empty. Moose are to be found on the same waters, and in the summer season, if approached very slowly and quietly, especially in a canoe, they show little fear of man. Last summer, as I stole down the thoroughfare into Matagammon, a cow moose and her calf loomed up before me in the narrow stream. I watched her awhile silently, noting her curious way of feeding, — now pulling up a bite of lush water-grass, now stretching her neck and her great muffle to sweep off a mouthful of water-maple leaves, first one then the other, like a boy with two apples; while the calf nosed along the shore and paid no attention to the canoe, which he saw perfectly but which his mother did not see. After watching them a few minutes I edged across to the opposite bank and drifted down to see if it were possible to pass without disturbing them. The calf was busy with something on the bank, the mother deep in the water-grass as I drifted by, sitting low in the canoe. She saw me when abreast of her, and after watching me a moment in astonishment turned again to her feeding. Then I turned the canoe slowly and lay to leeward of them, within ten yards, watching every significant motion. The calf was nearer to me now, and the mother by a silent command brought him back and put him on the side away from me; but the little fellow's curiosity was aroused by the prohibition, and he kept peeking under his mother's belly, or twisting his head around over her hocks, to see who I was and what I was doing. But there was no fear manifest, and I backed away slowly at last and left them feeding just where I had found them.

In curious contrast was the next meeting. It was on the little beaver stream below Hay Lake, a spot as wild as any dream of Doré, and a famous feeding-ground for moose and deer. I was fishing for trout when a mother moose came up-stream among the bilberry and alder bushes. I had stopped casting and sat low in my canoe, and she did not see me until abreast of me, within twenty feet. Then she swung her huge head carelessly in my direction, and went on as if I were of no more account than one of the beaver houses on the shore. Ten steps behind her came a calf. The leaves had scarcely closed on her flanks when he put his head out of the bushes and came plump upon me. With a squeal and a jump like a startled deer he plunged away through the bushes, and I heard the mother swing round in a crashing circle to find him and to know what had frightened him. Ten minutes later, as I sat very still in the same spot, a huge head was thrust out of the bushes where the calf had disappeared. Below it, pressing close against his mother's side, was the head of the little one, looking out again at the thing that had frightened him. He had brought her back to see, and was now plainly asking *What is it, mother? what is it?* though there was never a sound uttered. And there they stayed for a full minute, while none of us moved a muscle, before they drew back silently and disappeared, leaving only a double line of waving, quivering bush tops, like the trail of a

huge snake, to tell me where they had gone. On the same stream I got the famous bull of the expedition. I was paddling along silently when I turned a bend, and a huge dark bulk loomed suddenly out of the water dead ahead of the canoe. In front of the dark bulk two great antlers, the biggest I ever saw in Maine, reached up and out. The rest of his head was under water groping for lily roots, and my first exultant thought was that one might drive the canoe between the tips of those great antlers without touching them, so big and wide were they. Instead I sent the canoe swiftly forward till his head began to come up, when I crouched low and watched him, so near that every changing expression of his huge face and keen little eyes was seen perfectly without my glasses. He saw me instantly and dropped the root he had pulled up, and his lower jaw remained hanging in his intense wonder. Not so much who I was, but how on earth I got there so silently seemed to be the cause of his wonder. He took a slow step or two in my direction, his ears set

"Lunged away at a
terrific pace"

forward stiffly and his eyes shining as he
watched me keenly for the slightest motion.
Then he waded out leisurely, climbed the
bank, which was here steep, and disappeared
in the woods. As he vanished I followed
him, close behind, and watched his way of
carrying his huge antlers and lifting his legs
with a high step, like a Shanghai rooster,
over the windfalls. Of all the moose that I
have ever followed, this was the only one
whose head seemed too heavy for comfort.
He carried it low, and nursed his wide antlers
tenderly among the tree trunks and alder
stems. They were still in the velvet, and no
doubt the rude scraping of the rough branches
made him wince unless he went softly. At
last, finding that I was close at his heels, he
turned for another look at me; but I slipped
behind a friendly tree until I heard him move
on, when I followed him again. Some suspicion of the thing that was on his trail, or it
may be some faint eddy of air with the danger smell in it, reached him then; he laid his
great antlers back on his shoulders, moose
fashion, and lunged away at a terrific pace

through the woods. I could fancy his teeth gritting and his eyes at squint as some snapping branch whacked his sensitive antlers and made him grunt with the pain of it. But the fear behind was all-compelling, and in a moment I had lost him in the shadow and silence of the big woods.

It was that same night, I think, — for my notes make no change of time or place, — that I had another bit of this hunting which fills one's soul with peace and gives him a curious sense of understanding the thoughts and motives of the Wood Folk. I was gliding along in my canoe in the late twilight over still water, in the shadow of the wild high meadow-grass, when a low quacking and talking of wild ducks came to my ears. I pushed the canoe silently into the first open bogan in the direction of the sounds till I was so near that I dared not go another foot, when I rose up cautiously and peered over the grass tops. There were perhaps thirty or forty of the splendid birds — four or five broods at least, and each brood led by its careful mother — that had gathered here for the first time from the surrounding ponds where they had been hatched. For two or three days past I had noticed the young broods flying about, exercising their wings in preparation for the long autumn flights. Now they were all gathered on a dry mud-flat surrounded by tall grass, playing together and evidently getting acquainted. In the middle of the flat were two or three tussocks on which the grass had been trampled and torn down. There was always a duck on each of these tussocks, and below him were four or five more that were plainly trying to get up; but the top was small and had room for but one, and there was a deal of quacking and good-natured scrambling for the place of vantage. It was a game, plainly enough, for while the birds below were trying to get up the little fellow on top was doing his best to keep them down. Other birds scampered in pairs from one side of the flat to the other; and there was one curious procession,

or race, — five or six birds that started abreast and very slowly, and ended with a rush and a headlong dive into the grasses of the opposite shore. Here and there about the edges of the playground an old mother bird sat on a tussock and looked down on the wild unconscious play, wiggling her tail in satisfaction and anon stretching her neck to look and listen watchfully. The voices of the playing birds were curiously low and subdued, reminding me strongly of some Indian children that I had once seen playing. At times the quacking had a faint ventriloquous effect, seeming to come from far away, and again it ceased absolutely at a sign from some watchful mother, though the play went steadily on, as if even in their play they must be mindful of the enemies that were watching and listening everywhere to catch them.

As I rose a bit higher to see some birds that were very near me but screened by the meadow-grass, my foot touched a paddle and rattled it slightly. A single quack, different from all others, followed instantly, and every bird stopped just where he was and stretched his neck high to listen. One mother bird saw me, though I could not tell which one it was until she slipped down from her bog and waddled bravely across in my direction. Then a curious thing happened, which I have often seen and wondered at among gregarious birds and animals. A signal was given, but without any sound that my ears could detect in the intense twilight stillness. It was as if a sudden impulse had been sent out like an electric shock to every bird in the large flock. At the same instant every duck crouched and sprang; the wings struck down sharply; the flock rose together as if flung up from a pigeon trap, and disappeared with a rush of wings and a hoarse tumult of quacking that told every creature on the great marsh that danger was afoot. Wings flapped loudly here and there; bitterns squawked; herons croaked; a spike buck whistled and jumped close at hand; a passing musquash went down with a slap of his tail and a plunge like a falling rock. Then silence settled over the marsh again, and there was not a sound to tell what Wood Folk were abroad in the still night, nor what business or pleasure occupied them.

Formerly caribou might be found on these same waterways, and they are the most curious and interesting game that can be hunted without a gun; but years ago a grub destroyed all the larches on which the wandering woodland caribou depend largely for food. The deer, which are already as many as the country can support in winter, take care of the rest of the good browse, so that there was nothing left for the caribou but to cross over the line into New Brunswick, where larches are plenty and where there is an abundance of the barren moss that can be dug up out of the snow. Better still, if one is after caribou, is the great wilderness of northern Newfoundland, where the caribou spend the summer and where from a mountain top one may count hundreds of the splendid animals scattered over the country below in every direction. And hunting them so, with the object of finding out the secrets of their curious lives, —why, for instance, each herd often chooses its own burying-ground, or why a bull caribou loves to pound a hollow stump for hours at a time, — this is, to my mind, infinitely better sport than the hunt for a head where one waylays them on their paths of migration, the paths that have been sacred for untold generations, and shoots them down as they pass like tame cattle.

To the hunter without a gun there is no close season on any game, and a doe and her fawns are better hunting than a ten-point buck. By land or water he is always ready; there are no labors for effects, except what he chooses to impose upon himself; no disappointments are possible, for whether his game be still or on the jump, shy as a wilderness raven or full of curiosity as a blue jay, he always finds something to stow away in his heart in the place where he keeps things that he loves to remember. All is fish that comes into his net, and everything is game that catches the glance of his eye in earth or air or water. Now it is the water-spiders — skaters the boys call them — that play a curious game among the grass stems, and that have more wonderful habits than the common balloon spiders which sometimes turned Jonathan Edwards' thoughts from the stern, unlovable God of his theology to the patient, care-taking Servant of the universe that some call Force, and others Law, and that one who knew Him called The Father, alike among the lilies of the field and in the cities of men. Now it is an otter and her cubs playing on the surface, that sink when they see you and suddenly come up near your canoe, like a log shot up on end, and with half their bodies out of water to see better say *w-h-e-e-e-yew!* like a baby seal to express their wonder at such a queer thing in the water. Now it is a mother loon taking her young on her back as they leave the eggs, and carrying them around the lake awhile to dry them thoroughly in the sun before she dives from under them and wets them for the first time; and you must follow a long while before you find out why. Now it is a bear and her cubs — I watched three of them for an hour or more, one afternoon, as they gathered blueberries. At first they champed them from the bushes, stems, leaves and all, just as they grew. Again, when they found a good bush, a little one with lots of berries, they would bite it off close to the ground, or tear it up by the roots, and then taking it by the stem with both paws would pull it through their mouths from one side to the other, stripping off every berry and throwing the useless bush away. Again they would strike the bushes with their paws, knocking off a shower of the ripest berries, and then scrape them all together very carefully into a pile and gobble them down at a single mouthful. And whenever, in wandering about after a good bush, one of the cubs spied the other busy at an unusually good find, it gave one a curious remembrance of his own boyhood to see the little fellow rush up whimpering to get his share before all the bushes should be stripped clean.

That was good hunting. It made one glad to let even this rare prowler of the woods go in peace. And that suggests the very best thing that can be said for the hunter without a gun:—"The wilderness and the solitary place shall be glad for him," for something of the gentle spirit of Saint Francis comes with him, and when he goes he leaves no pain .nor death nor fear of man behind him.

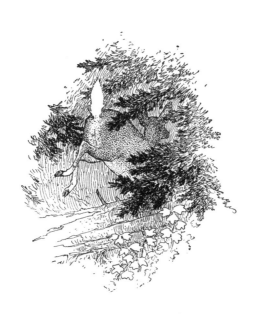

Glossary of Indian Names

Cheokhes, *chē-ok-hĕs'*, the mink.

Cheplahgan, *chep-lâh'gan*, the bald eagle.

Ch'geegee-lokh-sis, *ch'gee-gee'lock-sis*, the chickadee.

Chigwooltz, *chig-wooltz'*, the bullfrog.

Clóte Scarpe, a legendary hero, like Hiawatha, of the Northern Indians. Pronounced variously, Clote Scarpe, Groscap, Gluscap, etc.

Commoosie, *com-moo-sie'*, a little shelter, or hut, of boughs and bark.

Deedeeaskh, *dee-dee'ask*, the blue jay.

Eleemos, *el-ee'mos*, the fox.

Hawahak, *hâ-wâ-hăk'*, the hawk.

Hukweem, *huk-weem'*, the great northern diver, or loon.

Ismaques, *iss-mâ-ques'*, the fish-hawk.

Kagax, *kăg'ăx*, the weasel.

Kakagos, *kâ-kâ-gŏs'*, the raven.

K'dunk, *k'dunk'*, the toad.

Keeokuskh, *kee-o-kusk'*, the muskrat.

Keeonekh, *kee'o-nek*, the otter.

Killooleet, *kil'loo-leet*, the white-throated sparrow.

Kookooskoos, *koo-koo-skoos'*, the great horned owl.

Koskomenos, *kŏs'kŏm-e-nŏs'*, the kingfisher.

Kupkawis, *cup-ka'wis*, the barred owl.

Kwaseekho, *kwä-seek'ho*, the sheldrake.

Lhoks, *locks*, the panther.

Malsun, *măl'sun*, the wolf.

Meeko, *meek'ō*, the red squirrel.

Megaleep, *meg'ă-leep*, the caribou.

Milicete, *mil'ĭ-cete*, the name of an Indian tribe; written also Malicete.

Mitches, *mit'chĕs*, the birch partridge, or ruffed grouse.

Moktaques, *mok-tă'ques*, the hare.

Mooween, *moo-ween'*, the black bear.

Mooweesuk, *moo-wee'suk*, the coon.

Musquash, *mus'quăsh*, the muskrat.

Nemox, *nĕm'ox*, the fisher.

Pekompf, *pē-kompf'*, the wildcat.

Pekquam, *pek-wăm'*, the fisher.

Quoskh, *quoskh*, the blue heron.

Seksagadagee, *sek'să-gā-dă'gee*, the Canada grouse, or spruce partridge.

Skooktum, *skook'tum*, the trout.

Tookhees, *tŏk'hees*, the woodmouse.

Umquenawis, *um-que-nă'wis*, the moose.

Unk Wunk, *unk' wunk*, the porcupine.

Upweekis, *up-week'iss*, the Canada lynx.

Whitooweek, *whit-oo-week'*, the woodcock.